BODYSHOCK

BODYSHOCK

The truth about changing sex

Liz Hodgkinson

COLUMBUS BOOKS
LONDON

For Judy Cousins
in affection and gratitude

First published in Great Britain in 1987 by
Columbus Books Limited
19-23 Ludgate Hill, London EC4M 7PD

British Library Cataloguing in Publication Data
Hodgkinson, Liz
  Bodyshock: the truth about changing sex.
  1. Sex change
  I. Title
  616.85'83   RC560.C4
  ISBN 0-86287-317-7

Phototypeset by Falcon Graphic Art Ltd
Wallington, Surrey

Printed and bound by
The Guernsey Press, Guernsey, CI

Contents

Introduction

Over the past few years the phenomenon of transsexuality, the condition which makes people sincerely believe they have been born into the wrong sex, has excited interest and a large amount of horrified fascination.

From time to time newspaper stories have appeared about people who have supposedly changed their sex: who were once men but are now living permanently as women, and *vice versa*. In what way have they altered themselves? And, perhaps more important, *why* have they done it? Have they really changed sex, or just had some bits and pieces lopped off and other bits and pieces grafted on? What does it mean when somebody is said to have changed his or her sex? Could it happen to anybody?

Every time such a story appears, wonderment increases. What are these people who want to change their sex really like? After all, it is something most of us would never even consider for a minute. Nor would we want to. Whatever the difficulties and problems perceived in being a woman or a man, few of us would seriously contemplate changing over, even if this could be achieved without surgery or lengthy medical treatment.

But there is no doubt that a certain proportion of people do want to change their sex, and will go to literally any lengths to achieve this. They will spend any amount of money, put themselves through any amount of discomfort and pain, and risk losing their livelihood, families and friends.

Transsexuality itself is not a new condition. It has probably existed since the beginning of time and certainly all ancient mythologies contain examples of those who have apparently changed their sex. The main reason why the subject has created such interest in recent years is that it is now possible to do something about the condition.

Advances in understanding of sex hormones and also in plastic surgery mean that those who believe they have been born into the wrong sex can now be constructed into realistic approximations of the other gender. Before such treatment was available, those who felt trapped in the wrong body (as transsexuality is usually defined) had little choice but to put up with it. They could, if they chose, wear the clothes of the opposite sex and pretend they belonged to that sex, but underneath their bodies would be unchanged.

It is now possible to have a series of operations to lose the outward characteristics of one sex and acquire those of the other gender. Then the transsexual can live in the desired sex for the rest of his or her life, and nobody need be any the wiser.

Though many transsexuals have written their autobiographies – from the racy and sensational (April Ashley) to the sensitive and poetic (Jan Morris), with many more or less turgid tomes in between – the general public remains mystified as to the causes of the condition. Are these people physically normal, or aren't they proper men and women in the first place? Or are they suffering from some kind of mental illness?

The difficulty in understanding the condition is compounded by the fact that most ordinary people would like nothing less than to acquire the organs of the opposite sex, and this makes it hard to appreciate why anybody else might. However much women may feel they live in a man's world and however equal they may wish to be with men, most wouldn't want to grow a beard and have a deep voice. Though many men may consider that women have an unfair advantage of beauty, they would not themselves want to sprout breasts and lose their male organs – for most men a major source of pride and joy. But a certain proportion of biologically normal men do want to lose these organs. Indeed they come to feel in time that life is actually unlivable while those organs remain. Similarly, there are certain physically normal women who feel they cannot carry on living unless they can lose all their female attributes and acquire masculine ones.

This book is an attempt to explain why transsexuals feel

as they do, and why they want to make such far-reaching changes – some may say mutilations – to themselves. Many interviews with transsexuals are included, to show how these people have come to terms with their condition and how they have tried to solve their peculiar problem.

Transsexualism first came out into the open in 1952, with the sensational case of former American GI George Jorgensen, who had what is believed to be the first modern male-to-female sex-change operation, after which he became Christine, and a lecturer and celebrity in America. After Christine's story was published, scores of biological men all over the world wondered if they too could have the same treatment and thus become women. Gradually hormone treatment and plastic surgery became available, and most countries now have gender-identity clinics, which can advise those who believe they need to change their sex. Since the first operation, which was performed by Dr Christian Hamburger, sex-change surgery has made major advances and can be very successful. It is not possible, and seems as if it never will be, for a biological man to become a biological woman. Each individual's basic gender is determined at the moment of conception by the chromosomes and can never be altered. A biological man can never conceive children, or produce eggs each month. Similarly, a biological woman can never produce sperm. The changes that are made are basically cosmetic. They do not actually change the sex, but produce irreversible alterations which can look completely convincing. Today a man can have a series of operations and treatments which will make him outwardly quite indistinguishable from a woman. If a male-to-female transsexual were to undress in a ladies' changing room, nobody need know that she was not a 'real' woman. Plastic surgery techniques can remove penis and testicles and replace them with an artificial vagina. Hormone treatment can produce female-type breasts and electrolysis can remove facial hair. Hormones will also soften male outlines, and broaden the hips.

Sex-change operations the other way round – from female to male – have never excited the same level of interest, but they happen just the same. Partly, they have

9

aroused less interest because, on the whole, female-to-male transsexuals remain very quiet about what they have done to themselves, and virtually never seek publicity. It used to be thought that male transsexuality was far more common, and certainly gender-identity clinics see more biological men than women. Recent research seems to indicate, however, that although the condition is probably equally common in both sexes fewer women seek medical treatment. In many cases, they just decide to live as men without going for any hormone therapy or surgery at all. In fact, the first properly documented account of a sex change operation, in 1948, was from female to male, and was performed by one of the greatest plastic surgeons of all time, Sir Harold Gillies. Biological women who are convinced they are 'really' men can have their breasts and ovaries removed in standard mastectomy and hysterectomy procedures, and can even have an artificial penis and scrotum grafted on from skin elsewhere on the body. It all sounds rather mind-boggling, but it is no longer such a rarity.

Of course, psychiatrists and psychologists from Freud onwards have wasted no time in trying to explain this condition to us. Freud was particularly interested in intersexuality, as it was called at the time. Ever since transsexuality became a standard subject for psychiatry, many theories have been propounded. For a long time, the most popular was that the mother of the subject had wanted a girl – or boy – so badly that she then brought the resulting offspring up in the 'wrong' sex, so that the child did not know what he or she was supposed to be. The theory of a dominant mother and passive or absent father – once a favourite for 'explaining' the origins of homosexuality – has also been advanced to account for male-to-female transsexuality. These and other post-natal theories are now giving way to the pre-natal theory, which holds that something goes wrong with the hormones in the brain at the critical period for mental sex differentiation. This means that, although the child's sex is correctly assigned at birth, and the child is a physically normal specimen of the assigned sex, the brain and perceptions do not accord with the body shape. The mind, for some reason, is unable to accept the reality of the body.

It might be supposed that transsexuals, who persist in their delusion against all the outward evidence to the contrary, are mentally disturbed in some way. But they are not. In fact, if psychological tests reveal that a pre-operative transsexual is suffering from a recognized mental disorder, treatment will be denied. But if they are not mentally ill, what can be wrong? Surely it is not normal to imagine you are a member of the sex contrary to that entered on your birth certificate?

No, it is not normal, but it is not exactly abnormal, either, in the usual understanding of that word. The condition is extraordinary and baffling. It is all the more extraordinary in that transsexuals do not want to be as they are. They would give anything not to want to change sex, to be able to accept themselves in the gender that nature allotted them. The fact that they are unable to do this causes them and their families untold suffering and anguish. Only with the operation can release and happiness, a feeling of harmony, of bringing the mind and body into line with each other, result.

Many people, on reading stories about transsexuals, wonder: could such a thing happen to me? Might I one day wake up wanting to be a woman – or a man? The answer is no. All true transsexuals – that is, people who are physically normal and functional in their original gender – say that they have felt uncomfortable with their bodily sex ever since they can remember, and certainly from the age or three or four years. This feeling of wrongness never ever leaves them, but intensifies with the years. Unless the belief has been present since early childhood, the person is not a transsexual, though he or she may of course be suffering from some other kind of delusion.

But though transsexuality is so peculiar, and is still an imperfectly understood condition, it is not all pain, suffering and mental anguish. Most of the people whose stories are told in this book are positive, happy, life-enhancing people – at least, after the operation. All have remarkable, sometimes barely believable, stories to tell, even when they have not become famous in any way.

There is no danger that anybody can 'catch' transsexuality from coming into contact with such people. The condition is not hereditary and does not run in families. It is something which seems to come out of nowhere and there is no blueprint for it, no set of circumstances that would predispose to the condition. Nor does it seem to be on the increase. We hear more about it these days for two reasons: first, that effective treatment is now available, and secondly that people are more willing than before to come into the open and talk about it. Previously, it was considered a shameful secret, something to try to hide.

Comparatively few people are destined to be transsexuals. The current estimate is about one in every 10,000 of the world's population. The condition crosses all cultures and societies, classes and races. Anybody, from an uneducated peasant to the most elevated member of the aristocracy, can be born a transsexual. The condition is mental and emotional, never physical. At least, it is not physical in the sense that there is any ambiguity or question about the assigned sex at birth. Transsexuals grow up into biologically normal members of their original sex. Their sex organs and the amount of sex hormone they secrete are exactly the same as for anybody else.

Transsexuality has more than a voyeuristic interest for ordinary women and men. Those who have succeeded in crossing over the sex borders can tell us what life is like on both sides, something most of us will never experience directly. Transsexuals can teach the rest of us valuable lessons about the real differences between men and women, about often unnoticed or subtle sex stereotypes, about discrimination, about what marriage and relationships actually mean in our society. The present law in the United Kingdom – and in many other countries – states that the original sex remains the true one, and that nobody can ever change this. One practical implication of this is that a transsexual cannot get married as a member of the new sex. At one time, birth certificates could be altered, but now no alteration is possible unless a genuine mistake was made at birth. This British law was passed after the Corbett *v.* Corbett (April Ashley) case in 1970, in which it was held that a biological man, that is, somebody with XY chromosomes, could never be a married woman.

At the trial, April Ashley was told she could not function as a woman. She replied with perfect truth: 'Well, I can't function as a man.' There continue to be many anomalies in the treatment of and attitude towards transsexuals, and these shed much light on how we regard men and women in relation to each other.

Transsexuals commonly say how surprised they are at what they find on the 'other side'. Often, they have a very unreal picture of what life as a new woman – or a new man – will entail. Sometimes they are not prepared for the discrimination, for the stereotyping, for the expectations, that their new body shape and appearance will arouse. Their experiences illustrate in a dramatic way just how differently people are treated, according to whether they are perceived by others as male or female.

This book describes the experiences, both medical and social, of various transsexuals, and also gives, in layman's terms, a simplified account of the latest medical procedures available. I hope that it will go some way to reverse the 'kinky' image transsexuals still have in the public imagination and help others to see them in a new, positive and sympathetic light.

I hope also that feminists, chauvinists, traditionalists and radicals alike will find food for thought in reading this account of the many ramifications and implications of transsexualism, written by a non-transsexual who has tried to understand and come to terms with the unusual dynamics of this condition.

CHAPTER 1

What is transsexualism?

Most of us are fairly happy – or at least content – with the sex we are born into. Women may complain that they live in a male-dominated world, and men may argue that women, as the pretty and adored sex, have all the fun, and an easier time of it. But however much we may consider that the other sex has an easier and more privileged life, few of us would want to change places permanently, actually turning into a member of the opposite gender. Such a thought fills most of us with disgust and consternation.

But there exists a small proportion of the world's population – about one in every 10,000 – who are so desperately unhappy with their biological sex that they will do literally anything to change into the opposite. Mostly, these people are not neurotic, psychotic or schizophrenic, and outwardly they may appear perfectly normal examples of their true sex. Usually there is nothing wrong with them physically, either – they have all the outward and inward sexual characteristics of their biological gender. And yet, for some reason, against all the physical evidence, they are convinced that they are not true men and women, but the opposite of what nature tells them they are. These are the transsexuals.

Once considered an extremely rare and exotic occurrence, transsexualism now seems to be almost an everyday phenomenon. Though sensational 'sex-change' cases still make newspaper headlines, we have become quite used to them by now. At one time objects of pity, disgust or horrified fascination, known transsexuals now exist in almost every walk of life, as civil servants, entertainers, nurses, doctors, professional tennis players, artists, writers, computer consultants, university lecturers, teachers and housewives. Some have become famous, such as Jan

Morris, Renée Richards and April Ashley, while many, many more prefer to remain anonymous, their transformation a secret known only to a few close friends. These transsexuals live ordinary, respectable and quiet lives.

It is only over the past 40 years or so – since the Second World War – that surgical and medical knowledge has enabled physically normal men and women to be constructed into apparent members of the opposite sex. Biological men can now have all their male organs removed and replaced with a vagina. They can have breasts implanted by plastic surgery, and hormones will change their shape so that, outwardly at least, they can become indistinguishable from any other woman.

Biological women can, if they so wish, have mastectomies and hysterectomies and take large doses of male hormone to deepen their voices and make hair grow on their faces. They can even have an artificial penis and scrotum fashioned from skin grafts. If the conversion is cosmetically successful, as it often is nowadays, nobody need ever know that these transsexuals are not 'real' men and women. The one thing they cannot do, of course, is to reproduce in the new sex. There is, as yet, no way of giving a biological male ovaries, or indeed, any functioning internal female organs. Nor can a biological woman produce sperm and father a child. But who knows? One day even that may be possible. Scientists are now claiming that the days of a 'male pregnancy' are not too far off.

For the moment, though, a post-operative transsexual will be sterile, a castrated male or a barren female. The great majority of transsexuals would like to be fully functioning members of their chosen sex, but have to accept that, with present-day technology, that is just not possible.

Over the past twenty years or so, we have heard a lot about people who have supposedly changed their sex, so much so that it might be thought that transsexualism is a new phenomenon. But the desire to change sex is as ancient as history itself. The only difference is that surgical and hormonal techniques can now turn such people into a cosmetically acceptable version of the chosen gender. But ever since time began, there have been instances of biological men living and dressing as women, and *vice versa*. There are many references to transsexualism in Greek mythology. The goddess Venus Castina was supposed to respond with sympathy and understanding to those men who felt they had basically female souls. Another famous figure from Greek mythology is Tiresias, who, as a soothsayer in Thebes, killed the female of two copulating snakes. For this act he was changed into a woman by the gods. When he later reported that, contrary to general belief, the woman could gain far more pleasure from sexual intercourse than the male, he was changed into a man.

Stories abound of men being changed into women as punishment for some misdeed or other. When the Scythians plundered the temple of Venus at Ascelon, the goddess immediately turned all the plunderers into women, and put a curse on them, promising that the same would happen to all their descendants. And of course, in the Bible there are many references to eunuchs, castrated men who behaved like women and were traditionally keepers of the harem. Many eunuchs attained positions of great power and privilege from their special status as neither real men nor real women, and were often held in high regard, though some were considered to combine the very worst qualities of both sexes – bitchiness, slyness, deceit, greed and overweening ego.

Transsexuality also finds an early echo in the myth of Attis, whose priests were obliged to castrate themselves in deference to Cybele (or Cybebe), the earth goddess and consort of Attis. A poem by the Roman writer Catullus describes this myth:

> Attis with urgent feet treads the opaque ground
> of the goddess, his wits fuddled, stung with phrenetic
> itch, slices his testicles off with a razor –
> flint, sees the signs of new blood spotting
> the earth, knows arms, legs, torse, sans
> male members and
> SHE
> ecstatically snatches in delicate hands
> the hand-drum of Cybele, the hand-drum

of forest rites and Cybele's torture,
with nervous fingers taps the hollowed hide
shakes it and shaking summons the Mother's brood.

Attis castrated himself under a pine tree (so the story goes) and his priests had to do the same in order to serve the goddess. After castration, apparently, the priests became transvestites and performed traditional women's tasks. Some of them, according to R. Spencer, author of the book *Cultural Aspects of Eunuchism*, removed all of their male organs and became as completely like women as was possible at the time. In Catullus' celebrated poem, the castration is underlined by an abrupt and startling gender change. 'He' instantly becomes 'SHE'.

Most mythologies, both Eastern and Western, contain tales of how women have been transformed into men and *vice versa*. Witches and demons were supposed to have the power not only to change their own sex, but also that of anybody who happened to displease them.

In real life as well as in mythology, there are accounts of people in ancient times who were dissatisfied with their biological sex and who longed to change over. The Jewish philosopher Philo, writing about 20BC, makes reference to males who wished to become women.

Expending every possible care on their outward adornment, they are not ashamed even to employ every device to change artificially their nature as men into women . . . Some of them . . . craving a complete transformation into women, have amputated their generative members.

Suetonius' *The Twelve Caesars* also contains references to a 'change of sex'. The mad emperor Nero, after kicking his wife to death, was overcome with guilt and remorse, and set about trying to find somebody who exactly resembled her. Unable to find a women who would fit the bill, he eventually discovered a male slave, Sporus, who bore a close facial resemblance to Nero's departed wife. Accordingly, he had the slave transformed surgically into a woman. The mind boggles as to how this was achieved, but apparently the operation was successful, as Nero later went through a form of marriage with this man-made woman.

And in India, from ancient times, groups of men have travelled round the country dressed as women and behaving as women. Though physically normal men, they pretend to be female in every respect and, in this guise, go to ceremonies, weddings and feasts, where they demand large sums of money for bringing good luck. These gipsy-like males are thought to possess supernatural, largely malevolent powers, and unless given lots of money will steal babies and otherwise bring bad fortune on the gathering. They are the 'bad fairies' at the baptism.

In medieval and renaissance times, too, there are accounts of men living as women, and passing themselves off as genuine females. One seventeenth-century account tells of the Abbé de Choisy, who exhibited all the characteristics associated with present-day transsexualism. His mother, wishing for a girl, had dressed him as a girl and he had enjoyed playing this rôle. His cross-genderism persisted, apparently, until adulthood. At the age of 32 he wrote:

I thought myself well and truly a woman. I have tried to find out how such a strange pleasure came to me, and I take it to be this way. It is an attribute of God to be loved and adored and man – as far as his weak nature will permit – has the same ambition, and it is beauty which creates love. Beauty is generally woman's portion . . . I have heard someone near me whisper, 'There is a pretty woman'. I have felt a pleasure so great that it is beyond comparison. Ambition, riches, even love, cannot equal it.

Most books on sex change mention the strange case of the Chevalier d'Eon, who allegedly posed as a serious rival to Madame de Pompadour for the favours of Louis XV. Of course, as he had no recourse to surgery, his secret was soon discovered, but the king, intrigued, made him a diplomat. After successfully carrying out several diplomatic missions, dressed as a man, he retired to live permanently as a woman after Louis XV's death.

The earliest settlers in America also reported customs among the American Indians whereby certain groups of males received spirit messages telling them they were really girls. Ancient Tahitian tribes, certain African ones and also Siberians have cited instances of men changing into women and living thereafter as females. Like their ancient Greek equivalents, such people were supposed to be endowed with special powers, either to communicate directly with Gods and spirits, or to combine the wisdom and good qualities of both men and women in an intriguing whole.

Of course, transsexualism does not only work one way. There are countless examples, in myth and in historical fact, of women who believed themselves to be men, and who lived as such. First to spring to mind are the Amazons, the most famous group of warlike women, but all mythologies contain stories of women who behaved more like men and were respected for this.

St Joan of Arc, Pope Joan, surgeon Dr James Barry and Lady Hester Stanhope are examples of women who played out, for most of their lives, a masculine rôle, and very successfully too. In fact, when it comes to real historical figures, those women who exhibited masculine qualities were far more admired than men who adopted feminine behaviour. They were usually considered to be braver, more emotionally robust and also more intelligent than ordinary women. Queen Elizabeth I proclaimed that, though she might have the body of a 'weak and feeble' woman, she had the heart and mental powers of a man.

Although surgery and hormonal treatment to reassign an individual's original biological gender are comparatively new, the desire of certain people to live as members of the opposite sex has always been with us. Since the phenomenon of 'lifelong, extensive, cross-gender identification . . . is not new to either our culture or our time', according to John Money, co-editor of the monolithic work *Transsexualism and Sex Reassignment*, why should it currently be attracting such interest from the media, the medical profession, psychiatrists and feminist groups?

One reason, of course, is that it *seems* to be comparatively recent. It is only in the last 40 years or so that surgically constructed transsexualism has been a possibility, and that transsexuals have been telling their stories. The techniques, as they advance, have also been written up in the medical press. The earliest modern account of male-to-female transsexual surgery dates from 1933, when

Niels Hoyer's book *Man into Woman* was published. This tells the story of a Danish male painter who became surgically transformed into a woman and took the name Lili Elbe. Though the account does not describe the process in any real detail, it none the less records that the male genital organs were altered by surgery. The whole story is vague and highly suspect, in fact, and in any case the patient died soon after the operation, apparently of heart failure.

The first case to attract worldwide publicity was that of Christine Jorgensen in 1952. Christine, formerly George, was a physically normal male who underwent the first properly documented modern sex transformation to become a woman. Christine, who became an attractive and lively celebrity in America after the operation, is still alive and now looks like a completely ordinary, rather well preserved older lady, someone who may have been beautiful when young. She was operated on in Denmark by Dr Christian Hamburger, who published his own medical account of the case. Newspaper reports carrying the story encouraged people from all over the world to get in touch with Christine and ask exactly how the operation could be done.

The next case to generate a storm of publicity came in 1954 and concerned Roberta Cowell, a former racing driver. Roberta's story was serialized in *Picture Post*, a popular photo-journalism magazine of the time, and again aroused worldwide interest and controversy. Confusion arose because Roberta was not exactly a 'true' transsexual. Her book, *Roberta Cowell's Story*, published in 1954 by Heinemann, and also the newspaper publicity, tells how her sex was wrongly assigned at birth and was only discovered to be incorrect many years later. For a long time, she says in her book, she fought against the ever-growing certainty that, underneath the apparently masculine exterior, she was 'really' female all the time. I don't think Roberta, or Betty as she prefers to be called, would be offended if I were to say that, since the reassignment, she has not exactly been a traditionally feminine woman. She once said to me: 'If ever I married, it would have to be to a man who was more masculine than me –

and that would be bloody difficult!' Betty still likes fast cars, aeroplanes and anything high-tech and mechanical.

After the sensational – and sensationalized – cases of Christine Jorgensen and Roberta Cowell came more biographies and accounts. Georgina Turtle's *Over the Sex Border*, published by Gollancz in 1963, aroused some interest, but undoubtedly the transsexual of the century is the glamorous and humorous April Ashley. People who have met April express surprise that somebody so beautiful and elegant could ever have been male. Most male-to-female transsexuals (although not all) remain rather 'butch' in appearance, but there is nothing butch about April Ashley. She looks as though she could never possibly have been a boy. The fact that her surgery and treatment was carried out when she was in her early twenties may have contributed to this, but pictures of her as a boy show a fine-featured, wide-eyed, rather beautiful youngster. April was created a woman at great expense and with much pain and difficulty in Casablanca in 1960, by the world-famous sex-change surgeon Dr Georges Burou.

Some stories are imprecise about whether the people concerned are genuine transsexuals – that is, individuals who were physically normal in the original sex – or whether nature made a mistake. Though errors are sometimes made at birth, and babies with genital deformities may be assigned to the wrong sex, this book is concerned mainly with those who have no biological imperative to change. True transsexuals are people whose gender confusion exists in their minds, not in their bodies.

The publication of so many autobiographies of male-to-female transsexuals – there are, as far as I am aware, no autobiographical books by female-to-male transsexuals – has led people to wonder whether a person can ever *really* change sex. The answer is, of course, no. We know that functioning internal male and female organs can never be implanted into someone of the opposite sex, but reproductive ability is not the only criterion of biological gender. There exist many thousands of men and women who are unable to reproduce, after all. Women who have had hysterectomies, for instance, can no longer reproduce, but we continue to regard them as real women. Some men have vasectomies, or suffer damage to their genitals which prevents them ever fathering children, or they may have a low sperm count, or no sperm at all. But still we think of them as 'real' men. Though certain abnormalities at birth may make it difficult, sometimes impossible, for doctors to tell whether a baby is supposed to be male or female, the true sex is determined once and for all by the chromosomes, and these can never change. A male has XY chromosomes and a girl has XX. If ever the 'true' sex appears to be in doubt – and doctors at maternity hospitals say this is by no means uncommon – it can nowadays be determined by a chromosome test. In the past, of course, this test was not available, and mistakes were undoubtedly made.

Though men and women can now be made to look completely convincing members of the opposite sex, their true sex remains, for legal and biological considerations, what it was at birth. It was this factor which led the British government, in 1970, to stipulate that a person's birth certificate can never be changed, unless a genuine mistake was made at birth. Roberta Cowell's birth certificate has been so altered, because doctors were convinced that a mistake was made. But usually a transsexual must live with the fact that his or her birth certificate can never be changed.

Certain conditions – testicular feminization, Klinefelter's syndrome or hypospadias – can make it difficult to determine true sex at birth. Sometimes the sex organs can be so ambiguous that it is impossible to tell, and an inspired guess has to be made. If the wrong decision has been taken (and in the light of present-day chromosome tests this has become increasingly unlikely), the 'true' sex will eventually assert itself, usually in adolescence. This process can of course cause much confusion and upset, but these unfortunate individuals are not transsexuals.

In one sense transsexualism may be considered an incurable disease whereby an otherwise perfectly sane human being persists in the delusion that he or she is really a member of the opposite sex. Whenever there is cause to question the true sex, the condition cannot be considered transsexualism. By far the great majority of male-to-female transsexuals who have attracted publicity were physically normal males before the change. They may have been stunted in growth and feminine in appearance, like April Ashley, or they may have exhibited tendencies traditionally considered feminine, such as a desire to play with dolls. They may have enjoyed wearing women's clothes, and have taken every opportunity to cross-dress, but nevertheless they remained male through and through, capable (pre-operatively) of fathering children, though never of being a mother. The strong wish and urge to be female, and close identification with the female rôle, may lead some transsexuals to be mistaken for girls. This happened to April Ashley, as she recounts in her book, *April Ashley's Odyssey*. But April Ashley and all other transsexuals are biologically male in every cell of their bodies.

The same goes for the apparently far rarer incidences of female-to-male transsexuals. For some reason, there seem to be fewer women wanting to become men than the other way round. This may surprise those who consider that we live in a male-dominated world, and that men constitute the master race. Most gender-identity clinics, where potential transsexuals have to go initially for psychiatric assessment, report that the incidence is about four to one. We do not know for certain whether the actual desire is rarer the other way around, or whether it is just that fewer people try to do anything about it. What we *do* know is that many female-to-male transsexuals simply decide to live as men without having any surgery or hormone treatment at all. But from all the documented evidence available, it seems that female transsexualism is exactly the same as the male variety, in that most women wishing to change are completely physically normal in the original sex: the desire to change is in the mind, not the body.

Though transsexualism has, to a large extent, come out of the closet, awe, wonder and mystery still surround the subject. We can accept mythical stories of people wanting to change their sex, even that people of long ago and primitive tribes may have been possessed of this unusual desire, but many of us cannot understand why this should still happen. The mystery remains to some extent because of our failure to understand exactly what transsexualism is. Most psychologists and psychiatrists define the condition as a fixed and unalterable belief, against all evidence to the contrary, that one actually *is* a member of the opposite sex. Transsexualism is not merely a wish to become a person of the opposite gender, but a firmly-held conviction that one already is, and has somehow been born into the wrong kind of body. There is no 'cure' for transsexualism, though many therapies have been tried. It is true that a small proportion of transsexuals manage to come to terms with themselves as they are, and decide not to pursue surgery or any other kind of reassignment treatment. But they are in the great minority. Most say that they wake up every day, look in the mirror and are surprised at what they see. An alien body and face – their own – stares back at them, a face and a body that they consider do not belong to them.

Another reason why transsexualism has aroused more interest in recent years is because it is now possible to do something about the condition in practical (medical) terms. The main pioneer in modern transsexual studies was the late Dr Harry Benjamin, whose book *The Transsexual Phenomenon*, published in 1966, was the first attempt by a practising physician to shed light on the peculiarity. Dr Benjamin addressed the question of why transsexualism should persist in apparently equal proportions throughout the world. Why should some people wish to change their sex – but not others? Why were most people content to remain members of their original sex, while a small number were not? The phenomenon did not seem to be related in any way to cultural influences, the ways in which men and women were regarded in a particular society, or the way in which they had been brought up. For instance, throughout history there have been cases of girls being brought up as boys. Lady Colin Campbell, author of *Lady Colin Campbell's Guide to Being a Modern Lady*, was a recent example. In the house of a lord I once saw a portrait of a little boy, and was told that this was really a girl but her parents had been so desperate for an heir that they pretended their daughter was a boy. However, such a desire on the part of parents does not create a transsexual. Usually, when the child is allowed to reassert his or her true sex, he or she has no wish to be other than what nature decreed, though he or she may of course be disturbed in other ways.

Dr Benjamin and other doctors, mainly in America, asked thousands of questions, took extensive notes and documented case histories, then evolved complicated theories – but still did not arrive at any useful answer. After all these years of theorizing, we are still no nearer to knowing exactly what causes the phenomenon. It is possible nowadays, however, to describe the condition and to recognize it when it occurs.

John Money, another American psychiatrist, who, after Harry Benjamin, has probably done more than anybody else in the world to try to understand transsexualism, has described it as a state whereby the mind cannot accept the body. It was Benjamin who first coined the term 'transsexualism'. Previously, it had been known as 'eonism', after the notorious Chevalier. It is probably easier to say what transsexualism is not, rather than exactly what it is.

The condition has nothing to do with sexual deviations, fetishism or unusual sexual practices. Nor does it have much in common with those conditions which are often thought to be related, homosexuality and transvestism. Transsexuals do not become sexually aroused by contemplating themselves in the clothes of the opposite sex, as transvestites do. When they cross-dress, they feel right, more themselves than they did before. Indeed, the true male-to-female transsexual only ever feels at home dressed in female clothes. In a man's suit, he feels he is playing a part. In this, transsexuals are quite different from transvestites, who like to dress in women's clothes *purely* for erotic purposes. Transvestites are men who can give themselves erections by wearing high heels, blonde wigs, lots of make-up, low-cut dresses and padded bras, stockings and suspenders. Such men are fetishists, who evince sexual arousal from objects rather than from other people. Most transvestites enjoy cross-dressing only occasionally, and would be horrified at any suggestion that they should spend the rest of their lives dressed only in women's clothes. Transvestites are also proud of their male organs, and would not want to lose them.

Sometimes transvestites attend special clubs where they can dress up as women without anyone being any the wiser. Although transsexuals may attend such clubs, they do so to enable them to fulfil their deepest desires, in a way that will not arouse suspicion in others. But never for a minute does the male-to-female transsexual ever want to appear in men's clothes. He never, ever loses the urge to be a woman. The desire is constant; it does not come and go, and it grows more urgent with the passing years. Most importantly, it is not associated with any kind of sexual pleasure or arousal. Most transsexuals in fact have a very low sex drive and are far more interested in feeling comfortable and right than in being sexy or flamboyant. In the early days transsexuals probably did overdo their feminine clothes and make-up, and looked more like men in drag than real women. The present generation, however, usually dresses to be anonymous rather than to be noticed.

In fact, most of them say that their greatest pleasure comes from going out in women's clothes and *not* being stared at, rather than attracting attention. Today's transsexuals, in the main, feel happiest when wearing jeans and sweaters rather than overtly feminine clothes. They very often have short, utilitarian haircuts rather than long blonde tresses. The main blessing, for a post-operative male-to-female transsexual, is that the hated male organs are no longer there.

True male-to-female transsexuals are not usually homosexuals. As men, the vast majority go out with and are attracted to women. Many marry and become fathers. This causes immense problems, of course, when they come to change over, as they have to get divorced and, very often, lose contact with their families.

As a condition, transsexualism usually manifests itself by the age of two to four, long before the child has been exposed to any obvious sexual influences, and certainly before any sexual deviancy would be apparent. Transvestism and homosexuality usually emerge in adolescence, and often are not manifested until the late twenties. Many transvestites, for instance, do not become aware of their proclivities until after they have married, and have permanent access to female clothes via their wives' wardrobes. Homosexually-inclined men and women usually discover this fact about themselves gradually, often after they have experimented with boyfriends and girlfriends of the opposite sex. But the transsexual is different. He or she knows, as soon as any kind of reflective ability develops, that the apparent biological and outward sex is the wrong one. Usually this fact impinges itself in a kind of blinding flash, from which moment the conviction never disappears. There is a now-famous passage in Jan Morris's book *Conundrum* which describes how Jan became convinced she was a girl while sitting under her mother's piano. Rachael Webb, a more recent male-to-female transsexual, has described in an interview with me how the revelation struck her forcibly at the age of six. Judy Cousins, who finally changed over at the age of 53, after becoming a soldier in the Indian Army, marrying and fathering three children, has described how she knew with an 'absolute certainty' that she was a girl from the age of four. Transsexuals are people who do not merely wish to be members of the opposite sex: they believe they already are. As children, they believe that they will grow up into women (if male to female). The thought that they will one day be men is for them impossible to entertain.

Put like this, it might seem that transsexuals are suffering from a sad delusion of psychotic proportions. They must, surely, be slightly mad. After all, who in their right minds would seriously believe they were of the wrong sex, when no mistake had been made at birth? Yet the fact is that they are emphatically not mad. In every other respect transsexuals are perfectly normal, ordinary people.

Transsexuals are born, not made. So much seems abundantly clear. They come from all classes of society, from the highest to the lowest. April Ashley, for instance, hails from a Liverpool slum and never knew what a present was until her eleventh birthday, when her mother threw her a pair of socks. Jan Morris and Judy Cousins both come from traditional upper-middle-class backgrounds and Michael Dillon, probably the earliest female-to-male transsexual to have modern surgery, was born into a family of landed, indeed titled, gentry. Rachael Webb comes from a working-class background, whereas most current female-to-male transsexuals seem to hail from the solid middle class. Transsexuals are also found at all intelligence levels, though they do seem on balance to have a higher intelligence level than average. Very many have professional qualifications and have been to university. They are perhaps slightly more creative and artistic than the population at large, and tend to be loners. It may be recognition of their condition which makes them feel eternally alone – it is difficult to tell. Transsexuals are found more often among the self-employed than in hierarchical jobs, though there are a few in the civil service, usually at relatively low ranks. Apart from Rachael Webb, they are not conspicuously political or militant. Until very recently, they did not campaign vigorously for rights of their own. This is all changing now, however, as a growing number of transsexuals feel that present laws discriminate against them, and they are now more prepared to fight publicly for what they consider to be their rights.

Though some manage to form permanent relationships, both before and after the change, the majority live alone and carry out their new rôles with varying degrees of success. Jan Morris is perhaps the most successful post-operative transsexual of modern times, at least in worldly terms. Before her change, she was a highly-regarded intrepid newspaper reporter and travel writer; as James Morris, he was famous for attaining the scoop of reporting the 1953 conquest of Mount Everest on the same day as the Queen's coronation. Since her reassignment, she has gone on to ever-greater literary heights and achievements, becoming a runner-up for the Booker Prize in 1985 and appearing regularly on radio and TV. Avowedly and publicly asexual, Jan Morris has stated more than once that coitus is a rather tedious ritual which cannot begin to compare with the delights of art and literature. In stating that she is not very interested in sex, Jan Morris is probably echoing the beliefs of the majority of transsexuals. Of other transsexuals, April Ashley has largely lived alone since her famous, or infamous, 'marriage', and Judy Cousins, a talented sculptor, also lives alone.

As far as the law goes, transsexuals remain in their original sex. Though they can now have almost all documentation changed to the new name and designation, 'Ms' for 'Mr' and *vice versa*, the birth certificate cannot be changed, at least in Britain. Nor are they allowed to marry in the new sex. If a marriage is conducted and the partner later decides he or she would prefer a 'real' member of the opposite sex, the marriage can be instantly annulled, as if it had never taken place. When this happens, the transsexual partner is left with no rights whatever.

Though transvestites and gay people often join societies where they can meet like-minded individuals, most transsexuals prefer not to do so. Usually they shun any idea of a transsexual ghetto, and prefer to live and work in the community at large. One of the very few organizations founded especially for transsexuals, SHAFT (Self-Help Association for Transsexuals), is primarily intended to help people through the pre- and post-operative stages, rather than being in any sense a social organization. Overwhelmingly, transsexuals want to be accepted as completely ordinary, normal people and not as oddities, or as objects of pity, derision or voyeurism. They simply want to take their place in the world alongside everybody else, and to be allowed to live their lives with as little fuss as possible.

Over the years, psychologists have attempted to analyse the 'transsexual personality' and compare and contrast it with other deviants from the norm, such as homosexuals or transvestites. This comparison undoubtedly angers transsexuals, who do not see themselves as the slightest bit deviant. The latest such analysis is found in a book of essays entitled *Variant Sexuality: Research and Theory*.

Edited by Dr Glenn Wilson, a well-known 'sexpert' from the Institute of Psychiatry, London, where transsexuals are often assessed, the book contains a chapter on transsexualism which assumes that the condition is a type of 'sexuality'. The author of the essay in question,

Frederick L. Whitam, lumps transsexualism with homosexuality, and says: 'It is impossible to enter and observe homosexual subcultures without encountering transvestites and transsexuals of homosexual inclination.'

This attitude towards transsexualism further confuses people. For while it is true that some people who appear to be transsexual are found in the lesbian and gay world, the true sufferer from the condition is not really interested in sexual performance at all, with members of either sex.

In the brilliant film *The Naked Civil Servant* Quentin Crisp, a self-confessed effeminate homosexual here played by John Hurt, is interviewed by a bone-headed army psychiatrist. Studying Quentin's long titian locks, the psychiatrist quotes from the Bible: 'Male and female created he them.' After a pause Crisp, completely unfazed, says, 'Male and female created he *me*.'

Though male homosexuals and lesbians may consider they have much of the opposite sex in them, they have no real desire to change over. They enjoy their duality, and revel in it. Male homosexuals, particularly, are proud of their male organs and have no wish at all to lose them. Just how proud they are comes over in the playwright Joe Orton's diaries, edited by John Lahr. Such people would be aghast at any suggestion that they might have themselves castrated to live as women. For most, the idea would be totally repugnant.

The transsexual, by contrast, considers that the original sexual organs are actually the wrong ones, and wants nothing more than to have them permanently removed. Transsexuals feel that nature has played a cruel trick on them, whereas male homosexuals are very often inordinately proud of their bodies; many undergo body-building sessions to make their bodies even more masculine and muscular.

It is sometimes difficult for psychiatrists and doctors to know if they are meeting a true transsexual, an effeminate homosexual or a butch lesbian. The SHAFT handbook has, however, definitively differentiated them:

There are fundamental differences in outlook between the transsexual and the homosexual, a fact not always understood.

It is true that some transsexuals are experimentally homosexual before changing rôles, but perhaps the majority have led relatively normal lives up to that point. On the other hand, a transsexual whose identification with the feminine rôle is complete and who enjoys the company of men will positively not regard himself as a homosexual. The characteristic desire of male-to-female transsexuals is the removal of male sexual characteristics and the creation of female characteristics, including a pseudo-vagina, which will allow them to assume the rôle of women to the fullest possible extent, short of menstruation, conception, giving birth and lactation. For female-to-male transsexuals the desire is for the removal of female characteristics and the creation of male characteristics so that they can live the rôle of a man as far as present-day surgery will allow. The average homosexual would no more permit such surgery than he would the removal of a healthy arm or leg. He and his male partner value his male qualities. Homosexual partnerships in which one partner undergoes gender reassignment usually dissolve. If the other partner had wanted a woman, presumably he would have chosen one in the first place. After gender reassignment most transsexuals assume a sexual preference compatible with their new gender, though some do not. There are transsexual lesbians and homosexuals. It is a question of gender, not sex. Once experienced, transsexual feelings are unlikely to diminish either through the individual's own efforts or medical intervention. Indeed, such feelings frequently strengthen as the years go by . . . A transsexual is therefore faced with two possible courses of constructive action: to accommodate as best she or he can to life as her/his biological sex, or to seek gender reassignment. It is essential to grasp that for the transsexual this is not a simple choice but a profound dilemma: whatever path is eventually followed the predicament deserves compassion and the decision respect.

Even though Whitam, in his essay, appears to lump homosexuality, transvestism and transsexuality together as 'variant sexuality', he nevertheless makes some useful observations regarding transsexuality. He says that (male) heterosexual transsexuals often do not exhibit particularly feminine behaviour, and are found in traditionally masculine occupations. Before her change, Rachael Webb was a long-distance lorry driver, Judy Cousins was an army major and April Ashley a merchant seaman. In addition,

Whitam has observed, 'They are not given to dancing and performances and are not usually facile with make-up, costuming and coiffures.' This ability, Whitam says, is found naturally in the homosexually-inclined transsexuals. He goes so far as to say that heterosexual males are hardly ever to be found in occupations where make-up and dancing play a prominent part.

The (male) heterosexual transsexuals, Whitam further observes, do not strive too ostentatiously to imitate feminine speech patterns and gestures; instead they aim simply to dress and act at all times like ordinary women in the everyday world. 'Some succeed in this effort,' he goes on, 'while others remain obviously cross-dressed, because of their size or inadequate attention to details of the costume.' The main point that Whitam is making, however, and one with which most transsexuals would agree, is that the condition manifests itself in all cultures and societies. He reiterates the findings of other researchers in the field when he states that transsexuality does not seem to be affected by upbringing, sex stereotypes or the kind of society one is born into.

Transsexuals persist in their belief that they are 'really' men or women even when their physical size and shape makes this difficult for others to accept. For instance, a 6 foot 5, 15-stone, hairy-chested male, completely bald and with huge hands and feet, may still be convinced that underneath the unprepossessing exterior he is really a woman. Similarly, a petite woman of 5 foot 2 or less may be convinced that she is a man.

Transsexualism does currently seem to be on the increase, but that is most probably a reflection of that fact that because more can be done to alleviate the condition than at any time in the past more people are seeking treatment, and are therefore more open about admitting to their strange proclivity. Those who have researched the subject insist that the number of transsexuals remains constant. There is no doubt, however, that more than ever before are making the change-over. The indications are that over the next few years there will be even more, as the condition loses its horrific and sensational aspects and comes to be generally accepted as an incurable condition which strikes certain individuals, apparently out of the blue.

The Charing Cross Hospital, one of the few places in Britain where sex-change surgery is available on the NHS, has prepared guidelines defining transsexuality. Its leaflet on the subject summarizes it as:

1. A sense of belonging to the opposite sex, having been born into the wrong sex, and being one of Nature's extant errors.
2. A sense of estrangement from one's own body; all manifestations of differentiation are regarded as repugnant.
3. A strong desire to resemble physically the opposite sex and seek treatment, including surgery, towards this.
4. A wish to be accepted in the community as belonging to the opposite sex.

That is what transsexualism is. The big question is: how does it come about in the first place? What goes wrong?

CHAPTER 2

Why should anyone want to change sex?

How does the desire start? Why should anybody with a perfectly normal male or female body, somebody who is not schizophrenic or otherwise mentally disturbed, wish to have themselves artificially constructed into a cosmetic approximation of the opposite gender?

In the previous chapter reference was made to how transsexuality was, in ancient times, associated with almost supernatural powers and wisdom. Those few individuals who were privileged to bridge the chasm existing between the sexes were considered wondrous, special, people to be regarded with awe and respect. Now, however, most of those wishing to change their sex are quite ordinary men and women, not endowed with any special powers at all. Nor do they become so endowed once they have made the change-over – they continue to be ordinary, for the most part, unremarkable people. They are usually perfectly average, except of course for their permanent delusion that they do not belong to the sex that their physical form would indicate. For them, biology is most certainly not destiny.

I am not talking here of those unfortunate people with physical abnormalities, as they are not true transsexuals. Nor are men and women who wish to change sex for the sake of becoming more special and extraordinary genuine transsexuals. All real transsexuals know is that they feel very wrong within their existing bodies and that they will do almost anything to put them, as they see it, right. They are prepared, most of them, to sacrifice perfectly healthy flesh and organs, take alien hormones, risk losing their families, social status and career, and undergo prolonged pain, the equivalent of torture, all to achieve an ultimately unsatisfactory, and only partially functioning, version of their 'true' sex. Some will return to hospital for operation after operation, even mutilate themselves, and continue to make unrealistic demands of their surgeons. Apart from the pain and suffering involved, and the difficulties of maintaining secrecy (in many cases), transsexual surgery is also very expensive. There are very few surgeons either qualified or willing to perform the operations. Most do not like the idea of hacking away at a perfect, disease-free body, and those few who will agree and who are proficient can charge huge sums of money. Between £3,000 and £4,000 is not unusual for the actual conversion job, and often further plastic surgery is requested after that, at £1,500 or £2,000 a time. Male-to-female transsexuals usually have to submit themselves to years of electrolysis as well, to get rid of facial hair. Nothing else will do the trick. At about £15 an hour, electrolysis can cost £30 a week for two years or more (at least £3,120 on top of the rest). When you also consider that a stubble of one-eighth of an inch is necessary before the hair can be tugged out, you get an idea of how tedious and time-consuming the whole thing can be.

Yet, if you asked any transsexual whether the ordeal had been worth it, you would get an unqualified yes. Most transsexuals will tell you that they would go through it again willingly. One female-to-male transsexual who had recently undergone a bilateral mastectomy, a completely unnecessary operation from a medical point of view, as well as being the one most women fear above all others, said:

It is the most wonderful feeling I've ever had in my whole life. My doctor told me that many women would willingly give their right arm to have what I had – as luck would have it I was particularly well endowed – and I replied, I'd give my right arm to let them have what I've got.

My mastectomy has been the most liberating experience of my life. I can now run down to the beach in my swimming trunks and nobody ever gives me a second glance.

The fact that this particular transsexual does not have a male bulge further down has never excited comment. 'Nobody ever notices,' I was told.

Though transsexuals are usually happy to describe in detail how wrong and uncomfortable they felt all their lives until they had the operation, none can give a satisfactory explanation of how the condition arose in the first place, though most are avid readers of all transsexual literature, devouring anything that might shed light on their dilemma. Mostly, they admit that they do not know themselves why they feel as they do. 'The only answer one can give is that there is no answer, there is no explanation,' said one. Another told me: 'As far as I'm concerned, it's very simple. I should have been a boy, but though my mind was male, my body didn't become masculinized in the womb, for some reason, so I turned out physically a girl.'

Although few transsexuals can give a satisfactory answer, all have searched inside themselves, often for many years, to try to find the source of their cruel condition. Could it have been something that went wrong in the womb? Was it perhaps the result of upbringing, having an over-dominant mother and absent father, as has been seriously suggested for male-to-female transsexuals? Is it nature or nurture? Some transsexuals with mystical leanings have tried to explain their mismatch of mind and body in terms of reincarnation. A few feel that somehow their souls have got inside the wrong type of body, and others that they have to play out both a male and female rôle within the one lifetime. Other transsexuals dismiss this as a 'nice idea', but one which is so incapable of proof either way that it is not really of much use.

Those who believe that our personalities and attitudes are shaped largely by social conditioning have inclined to the view that the present wide polarity between the sexes is responsible for the transsexual condition. It has been noted in numerous surveys that parents treat babies quite differently, according to whether they are boys or girls. One famous study mounted several years ago at Sussex University tested this. Volunteer parents were given a selection of babies to handle. All of the babies were around the same age, but some were dressed in pink and others in blue. The parents were told that the pink-clothed infants were girls, and *vice versa*. In fact, some girl babies were in blue and some of the boys were in pink, but the volunteer parents were unaware of this.

It was very noticeable, however, that the parents treated the babies they perceived to be girls quite differently from the 'boys'. The 'boys' were handled far more roughly, talked to more and stimulated more. The 'girls', by contrast, were handled delicately, cuddled more and generally treated as far less robust than the 'boys'. They were also spoken to far less. Clearly, if such differentiation is made right from the start boys and girls are going to grow up very differently from each other. It should be noted that, in this study, the parents were not consciously aware that they made any difference between the 'boys' and the 'girls'.

According to the 'social conditioning' school of thought, society reinforces the differences between the sexes in a host of subtle and unsubtle ways. Boys and girls are, from the start, expected to behave differently from each other and to conform to certain set, preconceived stereotypes. Girls are given dolls and prams and pretend household appliances to play with, while boys get what are generally considered the more exciting toys – Scalextric, Lego, building bricks and computers. Then, to reinforce the stereotypes still further, boys and girls grow up seeing men and women perform vastly different rôles and, with few exceptions, see men in the lead and women as secondary and supportive, without much power in the outside world.

This of course is a crass over-simplification, but it remains the stereotype and is still potent. A certain proportion of people, according to this theory, cannot fit in with a preordained rôle. Some boys are happier playing with dolls, while certain girls hog computers and mechanical toys. As society does not, on the whole, allow these nonconformists to flourish, the only solution is to change the body, so that these pursuits will seem less peculiar. After their bodies have been changed, according to the theory, society will accept these misfits in traditional feminine or masculine rôles.

Those who adhere to this explanation avow that, once

changed, transsexuals become totally traditional people in the chosen sex, people who reinforce the stereotypes. According to this social conditioning theory, male-to-female transsexuals like to look and behave like Marilyn Monroe – the fantasy screen version, not the sad, alienated creature who committed suicide – and take an exaggerated interest in cookery, housework and other 'feminine' occupations. They also expect that one day a 'real' man will come and look after them. The female-to-male transsexuals, according to those who espouse the conditioning explanation, become ridiculously over-aggressive and chauvinistic, pipe-smoking, sporting beards and swaggering in pubs.

Anybody who has met transsexuals will know that this view is incorrect. For though there are people who become ridiculous parodies of their chosen sex, most are quiet, ordinary people in both appearance and behaviour. Wherever possible, they like to stay in the same job, or at least the same profession, and carry on much as before. 'I was always a feminine boy,' said one famous transsexual, Adèle Anderson of the singing group Fascinating Aida, 'but now I'm a boyish woman. I certainly wouldn't want to be the little woman at home, and I haven't the slightest wish to get married or have children – I've never wanted children.'

Karl, a female-to-male transsexual who works as a hospital administrator, says: 'I've never been aggressive or butch. So far as I'm concerned, I'm just myself and always have been. I would have liked to get married – as a man of course – but I long ago accepted that was absolutely impossible.' On the whole, male-to-female transsexuals remain rather 'masculine' and the female-to-males somewhat 'feminine', in that they are usually slim and boyish and rarely develop the machismo associated with the over-masculine man. (Physical considerations obviously have a bearing on this, but in addition there is the fact that, as children, they were usually treated as completely normal members of their biological sex, and so grew up with a certain amount of conditioning anyway.)

Though few transsexuals either way round are militant feminists, few can be called traditional, either. For the majority, their unusual dilemma has given rise to a singular way of looking at the world, and one which does not conform to the stereotype. They tend to be more tolerant, more humorous and more open-minded than very traditional people.

Another theory which has been put forward seriously to explain transsexualism is that transsexuals are people who have somehow failed to make their mark in their original sex. A man wants to become a woman, it has been claimed, when he finds he cannot make it as a man. Similarly, a woman expresses a wish to become a man when she has failed to attract men, or to be accepted in their world. If they won't accept her as she is, she will become one of them and join them on their own terms.

A few simple observations will reveal that this theory cannot possibly be correct. Some psychiatrists – male ones, of course – hold to the view that it is 'easier' to be a woman, and those who find it hard to make it in a man's world might want to descend the ladder, as it were, and actually go down the pecking order, because then nothing at all will be expected of them. The psychiatrists who adhere to this view are those who cannot understand why a normal biological male, the most powerful being on earth (in their view), should willingly want to have his male organs – the outward sign of his superiority – removed, and become a eunuch, a castrated half-person, neither one thing nor the other. The great majority of male-to-female transsexuals, however, have been 'successful' as men, in that they have usually held down jobs, obtained qualifications, got married and kept a home with their spouses. Mostly, they have been the family breadwinner. Many lead extremely 'masculine' lives before the change-over and succeed brilliantly in them. Most female-to-male transsexuals, too, have been 'successful' as women, though few, if any, go to the lengths of marrying and becoming mothers. The majority of female-to-males are not found, post-operatively, in extremely masculine jobs, but continue to work as secretaries, civil servants, teachers and lecturers.

Nor can you succeed in one sex where you have failed in the other. 'A failed man will automatically become a failed woman,' said Aileen, a male-to-female transsexual and SRN in a large hospital.

There is, it is true, a myth among some male-to-female transsexuals that they will be cared for and protected by a man once they change over, but this is only a fantasy, and until they let it go they must never have any surgical treatment. When you go to a gender-identity clinic, you have to show that you can support yourself in the new sex *before* having any irreversible treatment.

It's old-fashioned and unrealistic to expect that, as soon as you are reassigned as a woman, a handsome man will come along and take care of you. Apart from the extremely remote possibility that this could happen, very few transsexuals would even want it. Most would far prefer to be independent and self-supporting, and carry on as professional people rather than parasites.

A further theory that has been seriously advanced is that transsexuals are kinky people who either have sado-masochistic fantasies of being castrated or, if female, fantasize about possessing a penis and other male attributes – a permanent dildo. While most people, so the theory goes, are content to consign such ideas to the realm of fantasy, transsexuals try to turn them into reality by surgical mutilation. Again, this theory does not stand up to serious investigation. There are, it is true, some transsexuals who are masochistic, and who go in for polysurgery – operation after operation. Cochinelle, a well-known cabaret performer in Paris nightclubs in the 'sixties, was one of those who kept returning for more operations. April Ashley describes some of these people in her 'odyssey', but they are not true transsexuals. For the sexually kinky person, especially the one who is turned on by the surgeon's knife, there can never be any harmony, any satisfaction, in life. But for the genuine transsexual, once the change-over has been completed there is serenity and satisfaction. The quest is over.

But despite the fact that, so far, no convincing theories have been put forward to explain the transsexual dilemma, it stands to reason that there must be an explanation. Most doctors and psychiatrists who have treated transsexuals have agonized over the possible origins of the delusion, convinced that there must, somehow, be a 'cure' for the condition which does not involve irreversible bodily mutilation. Accordingly, they have maintained that if only they could get to the root of the problem, they could help the sufferer reverse the conviction of being born into the wrong sex. So they have painstakingly compiled case histories, asking about early relationships with parents, early childhood experiences and so on, in the hope that some common pattern will emerge. So far this has failed to be the case. Many tomes have been dedicated to the possible causes of transsexuality and years of expensive time taken up with counselling and psychoanalysis.

Most of this effort has been to little avail. Yes, the transsexual patient may say, I accept that my mother wanted a girl, and treated me as one; I accept that I over-identified with my mother and that my father was absent in my formative years. I accept all that: now will you please refer me for the operation?

For though over-dominant mothers and passive fathers (or *vice versa*) may raise disturbed or non-stereotypical children, they are not thereby 'turned' into transsexuals. Thousands, even millions, of children grow up in homes where the parents have ardently desired a child of the other sex, but this does not make the *child* wish to be the other. The parents' wishes and the child's rarely coincides in this respect. And by far the great majority of parents would be horrified to know that their child really believes he/she is of the opposite sex. Though they may have wished for the other sex, most parents want above all else that their child will be normal – like everybody else.

The evidence available so far points to the fact that, while mothers who want girls – and even treat their sons more like daughters – may predispose towards homosexuality, such circumstances do not create transsexuals. Few people now subscribe to the belief that an over-dominant mother is the precursor for homosexual tendencies in adult life. Like transsexuals, homosexuals are also born rather than 'made' by conditioning.

It appears that the most fruitful areas of research into the causes of transsexuality are those which examine pre-natal influences. The most likely explanation of the condition, from knowledge gained so far, is that transsexualism is triggered at some stage in the womb, and that the 'wiring-up' into male or female is not properly completed. Somewhere along the line a malfunction occurs which ensures that, though the body comes out correct, something has gone amiss with the mind. We do not know, as yet, whether it is something in the brain (which is, after all, a physical entity) or something which is non-material, such as emotions, attitudes, beliefs and convictions.

Recent work in biochemistry has shown us that non-physical aspects of humans, such as moods, temper and moral judgements, are intimately affected in the womb by the mother's – and also possibly the father's – diet and general health. Quality of eggs and sperm may, in the first instance, depend on nutritional and environmental factors to a degree hitherto unsuspected. There is already evidence that imbalances in trace elements, and too much lead in the system, can adversely affect a child's behaviour and learning abilities, and that the foundation for his syndrome is laid even before the child is born. It seems possible that transsexualism may follow a similar process.

This is not to say that the phenomenon has no social causes. Many influences impinge on personality, outlook and behaviour, and an incident which is traumatic for one person may be hardly noticed by another. It is reasonable to suggest that transsexualism may be exacerbated by society's attitudes towards the sexes. But from the extremely early manifestations of the condition, at average age three or four, it seems unlikely that it is caused *primarily* by outside influences.

As we all know, male sperm may be X- or Y-carrying, whereas the female egg is always X – female. An X sperm mating with an egg will always produce a girl, therefore, whereas a Y sperm will produce a boy. All the genetic and biological material needed to make physically normal males and females is present at the marriage of egg and sperm. We also know that, in theory at least, sex selection is now possible with *in vitro* methods of fertilization. A device known as a centrifuge can separate male from female sperm, and the egg can then be impregnated with the sperm of the desired sex. The system is not yet perfect, but it seems that the day is not far off when parents really will be able to choose the sex of their children. Whether doctors will agree to this is, of course, another matter. The point is, however, that eventual maleness or femaleness is determined, once and for all, at the moment of conception. There is no such thing as a 'neuter' embryo (or oocyte, as its technical name is at this stage). Maleness or femaleness does not impose itself later but gender is fixed at the point of conception.

Even those babies who are born without recognizable male or female organs will carry either XX or XY chromosomes or, very rarely, an extra chromosome of either gender. But any baby which bears a Y chromosome will be basically male, not female. There is a condition known as testicular feminization, whereby XY males are born without proper sex organs, and may be assigned and brought up as girls, their true sex reasserting itself later, when secondary female sexual characteristics fail to appear. Such people have, in the past, usually been wrongly assigned as females but now an operation at birth can put the matter right, and they can grow up as boys, which is what they are.

But though basic sex is determined at conception, all kinds of things can go wrong in the womb. Abnormalities may develop: hereditary problems such as haemophilia, dwarfism or muscular dystrophy may appear, or there may be disorders such as spina bifida, Down's Syndrome (mongolism) or cystic fibrosis; the baby may be born prematurely, or with a heart defect, or blind or deaf. But the biological sex is one thing which can never alter.

According to the pre-natal theory of transsexuality, although all embryos start off as either XY or XX, to all intents and purposes they are female at first. They begin to develop as females, and then the male sex is 'added on' at a later stage. It seems that the 'original' sex, biologically speaking, is female, and that maleness is something extra, something which has to develop positively. Embryologically speaking, says Robert Stoller in his massive work

The Transsexual Experiment, the penis is simply a masculinized clitoris, and the male brain is basically a female brain to which male hormones – androgens – have been added. There are critical periods in the development of the foetus, according to Stoller, at which the brain is particularly susceptible to the influences of foetal hormones one way or the other. It is these hormones which are primarily responsible for the orientation towards masculinity or femininity, however these concepts may be defined. In animal experiments, it has been found that too much or too little of the relevant sex hormone administered pre-natally has a dramatic effect on the animal once born.

A BBC *Horizon* programme some years ago focused on a strange phenomenon occurring in one extended family in the Caribbean, where some of the 'girls' naturally changed into boys at the age or 11 or so. In one family, the Batistas, four of the supposed girls had changed into boys because of an unusual hereditary genetic defect. This led the *Horizon* team to run a whole programme on 'the fight to be male'. What happens, according to the research referred to in the programme, is that the natural form of the human is female, and to become male involves hormonal interference with this 'natural' state. The 'fight to be male' starts when the sperm carrying a Y chromosome penetrates the egg. This eventually leads to gonads – at this stage undifferentiated sex organs – becoming testes. The Y chromosome activates the male hormone, which then absorbs the female parts which would otherwise turn into a womb. After this, the main male hormone testosterone starts to be produced. This thickens the spermatic cord and turns the foetus into a boy. The testicles have to produce a kind of 'maleness glue' known as H-Y antigen, which solidifies and finalizes the male organs. Unless this happens, they will revert to being female.

H-Y antigen, which is attached only to the Y chromosome, acts like a hormone and causes the gonads to secrete a substance known as 'Mullerian duct-inhibiting hormone' (MIH), which suppresses female characteristics. MIH is thought to be a large molecule which comes from the testes. In some foetuses, the H-Y antigen may not bind correctly, and in any case it has to compete with aggressive ovarian inducers. In physically abnormal babies, the wrong 'inducer' may have reached the sensitive site first. Testosterone, according to a report in the *British Journal of Sexual Medicine* (April 1980), is produced by the foetal gonad under the stimulus of the H-Y antigen. The author of the paper, Raymond Goodman, suggests that the best way of overcoming sexual orientation problems in later life would be to screen pre-natally, to see whether correct levels of the desired hormones are present. It is well known now that hormones, and hormone levels, can affect the brain, and also influence attitudes, though nobody yet knows to what extent.

Dr Goodman says, 'The ultimate answer would be to estimate H-Y antigen, testosterone and MIH levels as well as the genes and enzyme systems involved in the foetus and to correct any malfunction at an early stage.'

The *Horizon* team managed to produce for their programme one Mrs Daphne Went in support of the thesis that to become male is to win the fight in the womb. Mrs Went had XY chromosomes but her system was found to be unresponsive to testosterone, so she was brought up as a female. In her, the fight to be male had been lost. The *Horizon* programme dealt with physical consequences only, but there is a great deal of evidence available now to suggest that mind and body links are far more intimate than previously supposed.

'Roderick Random', a doctor writing in the *Medical Digest* in 1974, says that while it has been assumed for a long time that male sexual identity and behaviour are based on hormone levels, it is only just being realized that all kinds of things may affect hormone release – the weather, stress, diet and so on. He goes on to say that it is now beginning to look as though male homosexuality which, like transsexuality, is a mental condition occurring in physically normal males, may be based on androgen (male hormone) deficiency at the critical period between the fourth and seventh month of gestation. These are the times when the *brain* differentiates between male and female. By this time, of course, the body has already become physically and recognizably male or female. 'If this is so,' the doctor writes, 'then homosexuality is a biological variant with other factors added. In other words, sex may be in the mind but it is also partly in the hormones, even if the latter may exercise their influence on the brain – at least in the male.'

A paper printed in *Nature* (15 November 1979) stated that androgen receptors exist in the brain throughout the 'critical period' of brain sexual differentiation. The study, instigated at Harvard Medical School, found that androgens and oestrogens (female hormones) played a direct rôle in the development of rat and mouse brains. It seems that steroid receptors are present in the hypothalamus in the brain. In normal sexual development, there is a proper balance of oestrogens and androgens. Both males and females, of course, secrete a certain amount of the other sex hormone. Although the experiments described in *Nature* took place only with very primitive creatures, it is none the less true, as scientists are increasingly fond of telling us, that rats' brains are biochemically not at all dissimilar to those of humans. The *Nature* study found that peri-natal administration of DHT – a type of androgen – masculinizes certain aspects of sexual behaviour in both rats and guinea-pigs and affects the social behaviour of monkeys. Also, pre-natal administration of androgens can defeminize certain features of sexual behaviour in hamsters. The study concluded that its findings provided one possible molecular mechanism through which androgens may act as effectors of sexual differentiation. The *Nature* study was concerned with behaviour only, not physical characteristics. In other words, the experiments were carried out with physically normal rodents, whose post-natal behaviour was altered by changing their sex hormone levels. A degree of masculine or feminine behaviour can occur according to which type of hormone predominates.

One male-to-female transsexual, 'Cheryl of Battersea', a member of SHAFT, contributed these thoughts on the subject to one of the Association's newsletters. In an essay entitled 'Born or Bred', she offers the following possible explanations to the eternal question of 'Why?' The most widely held theory, she says, is that of 'learned gender rôle', which is supposed to happen before the age of five, and hardens with age. According to this theory, parents who wanted a girl but had a boy instead will subconsciously treat this boy as if he were a girl. Exactly the same happens, of course, the other way round. It is also possible that a mother's strong desire for a girl could, in the womb, trigger off the production of key hormones at critical stages, thus predisposing the eventual child to be especially responsive to a female type of upbringing.

Robert Stoller's classic theory, summarizes Cheryl, holds that the mother – who is perhaps bisexual herself – has an unnaturally close attachment to her son, and that the father is absent or indifferent. Thus the child grows up identifying closely with the mother, rather than relating to her. This is of course, as Cheryl points out, the classic explanation of homosexuality. She adds that by no means all transsexuals fit neatly into this pattern. In any case, it would not even begin to explain female-to-male transsexuality. There are very few, if any, examples of female-to-male transsexuals whose early childhood experience featured an over-attached father and an absent or uncaring mother.

The converse of the over-dominant mother theory to explain male transsexuality is that a dominant, strong-willed father and a passive mother may unwittingly produce a son who rebels against male sexuality to such an extent that he eventually repudiates it altogether. This, perhaps the furthest extension of the Oedipal theory, means that the son 'kills' his father by rejecting all forms of maleness, and 'marries' his mother by actually becoming her. Again, Cheryl points out that very few transsexuals fit into this pattern.

Chromosomal abnormalities, she says, account for a statistically insignificant number of transsexuals. Abnormalities such as Klinefelter's Syndrome, in which XY males possess an extra X chromosome and which gives a 'female' appearance coupled, often, with physical and mental retardation, is rarely found in the true transsexual. Most, she says, are normal males from a chromosomal point of view.

The idea that there may be some post-natal hormone imbalance is also not borne out by fact. By far the great majority of transsexuals have a completely normal hormone structure in their biological sex, as evidenced by the fact that at puberty they develop secondary sexual characteristics just like any other boy or girl. The research which appears to hold out most promise, Cheryl says, is the H-Y antigen hypothesis. Researchers have consistently discovered that H-Y antigen, which is present in all ordinary male skin and serum tissue, is very often absent in transsexual males. This antigen is, however, found in transsexual females.

A propos of this theory, Cheryl writes: 'This antigen is perhaps the genetic component determining to which sex future embryos belong, and an H-Y antigen malfunction decides whether some individuals become de-integrated from their biological sex.' However, she concludes, research into this is at a very early stage, and it would be dangerous to draw too many conclusions as yet.

Cheryl briefly mentions in her essay three other factors which have been put forward as possible originators of the transsexual condition. A number of transsexuals believe in reincarnation, and maintain that in their case a soul has unwittingly entered the wrong type of body. According to this theory, which is very ancient but as yet incapable of any kind of proof, the soul enters the foetus and, although it knows pre-natally that it is wrong, it can't then get out and enter a new body. So a cosmetic transformation has to be made post-natally. Most doctors and psychiatrists would view this theory as pure, unadulterated nonsense. And Cheryl remarks that all the research done on reincarnation appears to show that, if it exists at all, souls are completely neuter in gender and all take both male and female bodies. There is no such thing as a male or a female soul. Cheryl says:

Perhaps a traumatic incident involving fear and hatred of a particular sex in a previous life could 'explain' transsexualism. However, it is all completely speculative and of little real value, except that many transsexuals find this theory comforting. It enables them to put their dilemma into some kind of perspective, and also absolves them from direct blame in the matter.

The theory of repressed homosexuality to explain trans-sexualism is one that is often advanced. This, too, is rejected by Cheryl, on the grounds that very great numbers of transsexuals are either asexual or bisexual, and are not interested in partners who want sexual performance from them in their biological sex.

A further theory that has been put forward is auto-eroticism, or narcissism. Those who adhere to this idea maintain that, having failed to meet a real-life embodiment of some fantasy 'ideal' man or woman, the transsexual then tries to create that ideal in himself or herself. Here, Cheryl points out that most transsexuals wish to live unglamorous and anonymous lives, and do not wish to be flamboyant or be widely noticed by others. Also, she adds, large numbers have, before their operations, enjoyed close and loving relationships with spouses and children and do not wish to cause them distress. The change-over, she says, always involves a great deal of heart-searching and regret that old relationships may have to be severed, perhaps forever. Most transsexuals change over only when life has become unlivable for them in the originally assigned gender. For the majority, narcissism plays no part.

An interesting theory to explain male-to-female trans-sexualism has been put forward by Janice Raymond in her thought-provoking *The Transsexual Empire*. She avers that certain male-to-constructed-female transsexuals (as she terms them) make the change-over only when they have already lived their best years as men and see nothing but decline and decay ahead. She cites Jan Morris as the prime example of this. As James he was spectacularly successful as a foreign correspondent. When he saw, in his forties, that this rôle would inevitably decline with the advancing years, he gave himself a completely new lease of life by changing into a woman, thus getting the best of both worlds. Many women, Raymond observes, come into their own only after the age of 40, whereas male powers then start to decline, particularly physical ones. Male-to-constructed-females, she claims, 'hijack' the woman's part and pretend to be real, post-menopausal women.

Janice Raymond writes:

Another way of viewing Morris' acceptance and seemingly contradictory extolling of both [male and female] stereotypes is to say that Morris squeezed out of his male status all the vigour of young manhood. However, at the age of 47 – in the decline of his male vigour – he latched on to the status of a woman. Since women are often more vigorous when they are older and the cultural pressures have subsided, Morris captures the best of both worlds, so to speak. Transsexualism thus allows him to fully exploit both stereotypes.

It is certainly true that Jan Morris has been, if anything, even more successful as a woman than as a man. It is also noticeable that, post-operatively, many transsexuals do look far younger than 'real' women of the same age.

Janice Raymond, in her book, is not sympathetic to the transsexual dilemma; she sees it as the male way of gaining access to female creativity and, also, 'playing God' by creating artificial men and women by surgery and hormones. As men cannot create human beings in the way women can, she suggests, they do it by high-tech male methods. Female-to-male transsexualism Raymond views as primarily tokenism, giving the illusion that it happens the other way round when, in fact, transsexualism is mainly a male disorder. It is a disorder created, she says, by the male-dominated world of psychiatrists, surgeons and gender-identity clinics, with which resides the ultimate definition of what it means to be male or female. As a radical feminist, Janice Raymond takes the view that society's conditioning and sex stereotyping is ultimately responsible for transsexualism and that if sex rôles could become more fluid, less body-related, genetically normal men and women would no longer have this wish to mutilate themselves permanently. Raymond's viewpoint is convincingly and intelligently presented, but is disputed by the vast majority of transsexuals, who deny that they embody the worst aspects of the stereotypes.

Recent advances in biochemistry tell us that pre-natal influences have a far more long-term effect than has previously been recognized and since transsexualism crosses all cultural borders, and is found in all types of home and background, it seems logical to assume that some strong pre-birth influence may be at work. We may not know exactly what it is, but if transsexualism were purely a social maladjustment, one might imagine that it could be corrected by psychotherapy and counselling. As the condition remains notoriously impervious to this, at least for the moment, one must assume that transsexuals are born rather than made. If, as Janice Raymond suggests, counselling were improved and altered, we might see a change. However, that has not happened yet. Though the Johns Hopkins Hospital in Baltimore decided in 1979 to undertake no more surgical reconstructions, having concluded that counselling was just as effective, other hospitals and clinics have not followed suit, and the demand is as great as ever.

Whatever the origins of transsexualism and homosexuality may be, and whether they have anything in common, it is clear that the outcome is very different. For while most male homosexuals and lesbians would not want to be any different, most transsexuals fervently wish they were not as they were. Most say they would give anything to feel all right in their original sex, and all stress how much they hated feeling different from their classmates and friends of the same sex. Few homosexuals of either sex wish to be 'straight', while that is what transsexuals most desire.

CHAPTER 3

Surgical and hormonal procedures

Though the mechanics of sex reassignment may sound very mysterious, there is actually a straightforward procedure available for those who wish to live permanently in the opposite sex. It has been worked out over the years by transsexuals themselves, and by the doctors, psychiatrists and surgeons who are trying to help them or, as some see it, to frustrate their efforts at achieving an easy change-over.

Usually, as we have seen, people who wish to change their sex have had this desire from their earliest years. Whatever the evidence to the contrary, they simply cannot believe that their biological sex is the correct one. As the years advance, the conviction strengthens rather than recedes. Though transsexuals themselves may hope that with the passing years they will come to accept themselves as nature made them, in fact this hardly ever happens. For all, there comes a time when they feel compelled to seek treatment, and that life as it is can be endured no longer. So whom do they tell, whom do they confide in?

Before the 1950s, there was really nobody. A few surgeons in Britain, Casablanca and America were performing sex-change operations, but usually in deadly secret, and their services were unavailable to all but a very small and determined minority. Now, however, many Western countries have gender-identity clinics, where confused people can – in theory at least – receive counselling that will help them decide what to do, and, if approved for treatment, have their sex reassigned. These GICs are usually attached to the psychiatric departments of large hospitals, and referral normally has to be made by a GP.

The procedure that is now advised for all who are

53

gender-dysphoric (to use the ungainly technical term) is to confide in their GP and ask to be referred as soon as possible to the nearest GIC. This treatment is available on the National Health Service in Britain and at this stage will cost the patient nothing. Though the procedure is similar in other countries, the patient will, of course, have to pay where appropriate.

The gender-identity clinic will put the potential transsexual through a series of stringent psychological tests to determine whether the wish to change sex is genuine and whether it meets the criteria already laid down for further treatment to be embarked upon. The clinic also has to establish whether the patient will, after treatment, make an 'acceptable' man or woman, and to ensure that there are no deep neuroses or psychoses present which could render sex reassignment a frightful mistake. If the psychiatrist becomes convinced that the patient's wish is genuine, of long duration and deep-seated, the next step will be to put him or her on to hormone treatment. Once hormone treatment has been started, the pre-operative transsexual will have to live in the desired gender full time, and to be able to pass successfully, and in 'close continuous contact', for a member of the opposite sex, for about two years. After that, if all goes well, steps can be taken to implement surgery.

Hormonal treatment has the effect of masculinizing or feminizing to a certain extent, but will not by itself complete the job. Female hormones can soften a rugged masculine outline and help to develop rudimentary, more female, curves and breasts. The hormones will also bring about a measure of 'chemical castration', so that the male-to-female transsexual will, after a time, no longer be able to have erections, though all the male organs will still be there, of the same size and shape as before. After a time the pre-operative transsexual will no longer be able to perform sexually as a male. For the female-to-male transsexual, male hormones will deepen the voice and encourage facial hair to grow, help to develop masculine muscles and a more masculine outline. Outwardly the transformation from female to male may be quite dramatic after a few months on hormone treatment, but of course the female organs, both internal and external, will still be present. Menstruation will probably stop during male hormone treatment, but will start up again if the treatment is discontinued for any reason. Other changes, such as the development of facial hair and a deep voice, may be irreversible.

After about two years of living like this and experiencing a gradual change, the pre-operative transsexual may be referred for surgery to complete the job. For biological men, this involves removing the penis and testicles and creating an artificial vagina. Cosmetic surgery may also be carried out to enlarge the breasts, though this procedure is not usually available on the NHS. The end result will be somebody who looks exactly like a biological woman. If you were to see a male-to-female transsexual undressed, you would not be able to tell the difference; assuming that the job had been well done, there would be no giveaway signs. The surgical techniques, which began to be perfected in the 1950s, have advanced so far that the operation, from an aesthetic point of view, can be a complete success. Penile skin is used to line the vagina, and the post-operative transsexual can enjoy a perfectly normal sex life, as a woman, if that is her wish. Of course, the constructed vagina is a cul-de-sac, and there will be no female organs inside. Most post-operative transsexuals continue to take female hormone so that maleness does not start to reassert itself. As the patient is still biologically male, male hormones will continue to be produced, and must be overridden by female ones. After castration, however, the output of male hormone will of course be much smaller.

Though the operation is available under the NHS, very few surgeons are qualified to carry it out, and there may well be a long waiting-list. The other major aspect of male-to-female transformation is of course the removal of facial hair. As this is the most obvious giveaway, those who seriously wish to pursue sex reassignment are advised to begin electrolysis treatment as soon as they can. Unfortunately, female hormones will not remove facial hair, nor will they unbreak a voice. Speech therapy can help considerably with the voice. But while some biological women do have naturally deep husky voices, which are usually considered attractive, very few real women have beards. Beard removal is considered by most transsexuals to be the very worst aspect of the transformation. In their books April Ashley and Jan Morris do not even mention it, though one must assume they had hair-removal treatment of some kind. Electrolysis, the only guaranteed permanent way of removing facial hair, is painful and protracted, and because the treatment is considered cosmetic it is not normally obtainable under the NHS; it can therefore work out very expensive. About 500 to 600 hairs can be removed in an hour by a competent operator, but one shot of the needle does not always do the trick: two or three shots may be required to 'kill' each hair. Moreover, each individual's pain threshold has to be taken into account. Many people find electrolysis extremely painful, but as yet there is no alternative. Full and total beard removal takes, on average, one two-hour session per week for two years. There is also a very strong possibility of scarring, and the patient rarely develops the smooth skin of a woman. However, the important point for the transsexual is that after treatment there will no longer be any visible sign of a beard.

For women who wish to live as men, the process is in many ways less satisfactory. Although male hormones can give an outwardly convincing male appearance, there is no way that a biological woman can become a functioning male, even to the extent that a biological male can subsequently perform as a woman. The male hormones taken are more permanent and less reversible in their effects than female hormone, but the surgical procedures are less good. Female-to-male transsexuals usually have a bilateral mastectomy – often at the earliest possible opportunity – and a hysterectomy to remove their female internal organs and ensure that menstruation does not recur. But there is no operation as yet which can provide a penis and testicles of convincing appearance and workability.

Some female-to-male transsexuals have a phalloplasty: an artifical penis constructed from skin taken elsewhere on the body, often the thigh. As such, it is not made of erectile tissue and cannot perform sexually. Given that there is also as yet no way of constructing visually convincing male testicles, when a female-to-male transsexual is undressed the secret is out. Also, the phalloplasty operation is in many ways still experimental, even though the first one was performed in 1948, and cannot be considered truly satisfactory.

Many female-to-male transsexuals choose to live without external male organs, especially in Britain, where the operation is virtually unobtainable. They manage with difficulty when it comes to using men's toilets or explaining their predicament to potential girlfriends. But even with the limitations, most feel happier and more normal when living as men.

These, briefly, are the procedures and, stated thus, it all sounds plain sailing. But, of course, it isn't quite as simple as that. In the first place, there are few doctors anywhere in the world who are skilled at carrying out transsexual surgery, and most psychiatrists admit they are completely baffled by the phenomenon. Virtually all of the psychiatrists treatings transsexuals, both in Britain and other countries, are men who cannot for the life of them understand why a physically normal and seemingly intelligent man should ask for his balls to be removed so that he can live as a woman. As one male-to-female transsexual told me: 'They simply can't understand why a man should want to have his penis cut off. That somebody who has been bestowed this gift should want to have it removed so that he can live as an inferior creature, and not even a functioning one at that, is quite beyond them.'

Most of the psychiatrists who treat transsexuals have not studied the subject in any great detail, and many are not even particularly interested in it. They have very often entered the arena by default, as it were, and fail completely to understand the dynamics of the condition. In America, the subject has been researched thoroughly, mainly by Harry Benjamin, John Money and Robert Stoller. These three psychiatrists have made a genuine attempt to understand transsexualism but, according to Janice Raymond, they have got the whole picture sadly wrong. They have tried to play God, she claims in her book, and at their gender-identity clinics have simply succeeded in reinforcing sex stereotypes which, but for them, might have begun to recede. The leading American transsexual experts, says Raymond, have themselves defined what it means to be male or female, and those wishing to pursue sex reassignments have no choice but to go along with their definitions, or prejudices.

Many present-day transsexuals feel that the American model of sex stereotyping has crossed the Atlantic intact, and that the British gender-identity clinics also insist on fairly rigorous and narrow definitions of masculinity and femininity. Transsexuals soon discover that, unless they go along with the psychiatrists' preconceived stereotypes, they are unlikely to get any real help at the clinics. It is possible, of course, to bypass the psychiatrists completely and go straight to a private clinic abroad, but this is beyond the means and scope of most transsexuals, who, apart from not having the sums of money needed, are in any case confused and unsure of themselves at the outset. Also, at the initial stages they may not know exactly what kind of treatment they want, or what it entails.

Pre-operative transsexuals often find that once they have entered a gender-identity clinic they can no longer be themselves, but have to conform to how the psychiatrist sees a man or a woman. If they are men wanting to be women, they will usually have to wear skirts and make-up, have attractive hairdos and at least pretend to an interest in cooking and babies. That, for the average psychiatrist, is what being a woman is all about. One male-to-female transsexual told me:

Once I made the mistake of going to the gender-identity clinic dressed in jeans, and the psychiatrist immediately thought I wasn't sincere in my wish to be a woman. He said that if I wanted to pursue treatment, I must wear a skirt. He also asked whether I wanted to sleep with men, and whether I would like to marry and settle down as a wife. Most psychiatrists simply can't understnd why you want a vagina if you are not interested in sexual intercourse with a man. But for most of us the prospect of having sex as a woman is very low down on the list of priorities.

We just want our bodies to conform to our mental picture of

ourselves, and this is nothing to do with acting out stereotypes. There are as many different types of transsexual as of any other people. Some are feminine in the traditional sense, and house-wifely, while others remain masculine and rather butch. Not all of us are interested in finding a partner for life, or to be sexually active. But, in order to get the best kind of treatment, you have to pretend to be ultra-feminine, unintelligent and passive.

The SHAFT handbook states:

There is a widespread misconception that psychiatrists are sympathetic listeners who are there to help you solve your problems. In the context of gender reassignment this is pure nonsense. It is largely up to you to solve your own problems; the principal function of the psychiatrist is simply to protect you from yourself.

The situation is not much better the other way round. If the average male psychiatrist views male-to-female trans-sexuals with fear and loathing ('They fear it may be catching,' said one), imagine how they regard a petite, polite lady who walks in and shyly says she would like to be a man. The impudence! That a biological woman, a member of an inferior species, should announce that she really *is* a man, against all evidence to the contrary, defies comment. By implication, this little lady wishes to gain male privileges which, as all feminists know, are jealously guarded. Perhaps she suffers from a massive dose of penis envy.

The standard questions asked of a woman who wants reassignment to the male gender are: can you mend a fuse? do you know about car engines? how are you with mechanical things? The deadly sex stereotype, according to transsexuals, operates just as surely and insidiously this way round.

Female-to-male transsexuals may also have to try to be more aggressive than comes naturally, because that is the way men – real men, that is – are seen to behave. You can't be serious about wanting to be a man unless you behave like one, the assumption goes. In actual fact, by far the great majority of female-to-male transsexuals are rather quiet, retiring people who do not wish to make a fuss, only to pursue their unusual destiny with as little impediment as possible. For though transsexuals are totally convinced of their 'true' sex, society has often conditioned them into behaving according to their outward, biological sex. The female-to-male transsexuals therefore tend to be rather quiet and gentle and the male-to-female ones somewhat dominant and aggressive, wanting and expecting to get their own way.

Physical size is often another factor which makes assessment by a psychiatrist difficult. In her own cruel way, nature very often decides to make male-to-female transsexuals very tall and large-boned and female-to-male transsexuals very small people. The average height of the f-to-ms is 5 foot 4, while m-to-fs are very often over 6 feet tall. The physical aspect often underlines the psychiatrist's hidden conviction that these people are really crazy. They're not even an ideal size to live as members of the opposite sex, is a common thought.

However, the sheer determination of most pre-operative transsexuals makes them develop armadillo skins when dealing with doctors and psychiatrists. They tend to see the psychiatric assessment mainly as the first of many hurdles in their chosen obstacle race. If they can convince the doctor that they are not mad and that they will be immeasurably happier in the reassigned sex, then they can be recommended for further treatment. The SHAFT handbook states:

Once the decision to change gender has been made, the psychiatrist will offer the patient a certificate stating that the patient is under his care and that it is in the interest of the patient that he/she should dress in the clothes of the seemingly opposite biological sex. This certificate can be useful if the transsexual encounters any difficulties with the law.

After this stage is finished, the psychiatrist will then prescribe hormones, or give permission for hormones to be prescribed. These must usually be taken for two years before actual surgery. For male-to-female transsexuals the female hormone oestrogen is used. This may come in natural or synthetic form, but the main drug prescribed is Premarin, which is extracted from the urine of pregnant mares. At first, extremely high doses, 7·5 milligrams daily, are given, in the form of tablets. These tablets are coated so that they dissolve after passing through the stomach, which helps to prevent the stomach upsets that the very high doses might otherwise trigger.

Most oestrogens are gastric irritants. Stilboestrol is the most common synthetic female hormone used, and other synthetics sometimes prescribed are Ethinyloestradiol and Mestranol. All the time female hormones are being taken, the male hormones continue to be produced by the biological male. To suppress the action of these, an androgen-suppressing drug is sometimes used as well. This drug, Androcur, is not standard, as it has unpleasant side-effects for some people. It makes some individuals feel desperately tired for no apparent reason. Many doctors now consider that the benefits of androgen-suppressors are almost completely negated by their unwanted side-effects.

The trouble with taking hormones is that their effect can never be guaranteed in advance. When Judy Cousins was taking massive doses of female hormone, she noted down her new measurements and any noted side-effects day by day in a diary. At first she found progress disappointingly slow – for ages nothing at all seemed to happen. As with any drug, individuals differ greatly in their responses. It might be imagined that transsexuals, with their long-seated wish to be women, might secrete more than the average amount of female hormone, but in fact this is hardly ever the case. All 'normal' men and women secrete certain amounts of the opposite sex hormone, but the quantity is not greater in transsexuals.

However strong the mental desire for change, most transsexuals find that male hormones are produced and secreted as if there were no such conviction. The mind's desire has no effect on bodily functions, which seems strange. The male-to-female transsexual's sense of identity and femaleness develops in spite of his continuous production of male hormones.

Over a period of about two years, the male-to-female transsexual may notice the following changes, if hormone treatment is undertaken exactly as indicated: eventually, female-type breasts will develop, with enlarged areolae and pigmentation of the nipples. Very rarely, though, will hormone treatment alone produce breasts that will satisfy the patient. After all, as several doctors have pointed out, very many biological women have very small breasts, in spite of continuously producing large quantities of female hormone. In some cases, there is no noticeable breast development at all.

Oestrogen will also cause softening of the male outline, and will encourage feminine fat distribution to an extent. A more noticeable waist will develop, and the skin in general may become softer and less rugged-looking. Hairs on the head may improve in condition and thickness, but oestrogen will not cure baldness, or make hairs grow back on a hairline that has receded.

There may at the same time be some softening of facial and body hair, but it will not disappear to any noticeable extent. Some men notice that their testes decrease in size during the period when they are taking large doses of hormone, and certainly, in the course of time, sterility and impotence will result.

Oestrogen therapy has definite limitations. It cannot alter the masculine voice or stop the beard from continuing to grow. All body hair elsewhere which has made its appearance, such as on the chest or back, will remain. Some transsexuals say they notice psychological effects from taking oestrogen, and become weepier, more indecisive and more passive than previously. It is difficult to know, however, whether this is a direct result of oestrogen therapy, whether it comes from relief that something is happening, or whether the transsexual thinks this is how a woman ought to feel. Judy Cousins noted that there was a gradual change from being attracted to women to being attracted to men, though not all transsexuals notice this. For many, sexual proclivities remain entirely unchanged by hormone therapy.

Such massive doses of female hormones are not without their attendant dangers and possible side-effects. There is a small risk of thromboembolic disease, deep-vein thrombosis, pulmonary embolism and even myocardial infarction. The risk of liver damage is also slightly increased. Most patients, however, do not suffer adverse side-effects from this hormone treatment, which may continue post-operatively for the rest of the patient's life.

Some patients complain that oestrogen therapy weakens the nails and makes them break more easily. It has now been shown that there is a connection between taking high doses of oestrogen and an inability to absorb nutrients correctly from the diet. For this reason, present-day transsexuals are advised to take certain multivitamin and mineral supplements while the very high doses are being prescribed.

For the female-to-male transsexual, the reverse happens. Massive doses of male hormone – often given by injection – are taken to encourage the body to develop a male outline and facial hair and to deepen the voice. The hormones prescribed are androgens, steroid hormones secreted by the testes and also the adrenal glands. The main androgen is testosterone and this is the hormone usually given to women wishing to live as men. Its first effect is to act on the pituitary gland in the brain to stop menstruation – usually the most hated outward sign of being in the 'wrong' sex. Testosterone stops the ovaries producing and releasing the monthly egg. Under the continuing influence of testosterone, oestrogen production is halted and menstruation ceases quickly. It will of course come back if the hormone treatment is discontinued for any reason. Suppression of oestrogen release also works to produce certain male characteristics such as thinning of the hair on the head, growth of body and facial hair, and a more bony, masculine outline. As with oestrogen therapy, individuals react very differently to this hormone, and nobody can guarantee exactly what will happen or at what time. It may take many months of treatment before there is any beard growth – the longed-for outcome for f-to-ms, as breasts are for m-to-fs. Testosterone will not alter height or general physique, but fat distribution will alter as the waist becomes thicker and fat is lost from hips and thighs.

Some patients may develop teenage-type acne temporarily when taking testosterone, but this does not usually last for long. Testosterone does however bring an increased risk of heart attacks, strokes and even gangrene.

For this reason, female-to-male transsexuals are not usually advised to take male hormone for any longer than absolutely necessary, once irreversible changes have been produced. In view of the very real danger that menstruation will return as soon as hormone therapy finishes, most female-to-male transsexuals make up their minds to have a hysterectomy as quickly as possible.

The surgical techniques, which have been developed only over the past 30 years or so, are far more satisfactory for male-to-female transsexuals than *vice versa*. In the early days, the operation was horribly painful and protracted – Jan Morris and April Ashley, who both went to Casablanca, speak of 'cruel pain', which Ashley likens to that inflicted by branding irons.

Jan Morris, in her book, fails to make it clear whether her operation included the creation of a pseudo-vagina, but one assumes it did, as that is Dr Burou's speciality, while April Ashley's account of her operation in the hands of Georges Burou in 1960 reads like a description of the worst kind of medieval torture:

As the anaesthetic wore off, I became aware of the most hideous pain. It was unlike anything in my previous experience or, I suspect, in yours. It was as if branding irons were being vigorously applied to the middle part of my body. I screamed and a nurse came quickly with a pain-killing injection.

She continues:

The injections stilled the pain, but put everything else at a distance too, as if the world were taking place in slow motion on a screen. They did however allow sufficient respite for me to give myself a superficial examination. My middle was grotesquely swollen and bound inches deep with bandages into which blood continuously spilt and congealed. A rubber tube for peeing came out of it. Pints of sweat poured off me and this was exacerbated by the oppressive heat of the day . . . On the fourth day the branding irons descended and sizzled across my body and I screamed for the nurse. Instead of a jab she gave me tablets. The pain mounted and closed in on me . . . Occasionally my eyes lost focus and ceased to convey coherent information to my brain, and I would go into a semi-blind hysterical state which was usually followed by unconsciousness. I was soggy the whole time. It was delightful when they came to wash me, even though the refreshment was brief. Lightweight European meals appeared and were taken away barely touched.

What caused all this agony? In her book April Ashley remains reticent as to precisely what was done. She says that Dr Burou kept the exact details secret, but adds that she does not imagine his technique differs radically from that of any other transsexual surgeon. There are actually two kinds of operation available to a male-to-female transsexual. The first one is merely cosmetic, and includes the removal of penis and testicles but not the creation of a vagina. The other, more complicated procedure favoured by Dr Burou involves inverting penile and scrotal skin to form a pseudo-vagina. Needless to say, this second operation is by far the more popular and is the one usually requested.

The simpler, non-vaginal operation can be performed by any experienced plastic surgeon. After the penis has been surgically removed, the urethra is situated further down so that the patient can urinate like a woman. Some surgeons fashion labia to give the appearance of a vaginal opening, but this is not always done. Older patients, and those who do not wish to pursue an active sex life, may opt for this operation, which is virtually always free of post-operative complications.

The second operation, in which a vagina is created, is very highly skilled. Extremely few surgeons are competent to carry it out. Transsexuals are usually advised to go only to a doctor with a proven record of success in this field, as a botched job can be little short of nightmarish. It is essential that the vagina is created in the same operation as the penis and testicles are removed, because once the tissue has been discarded it cannot be used later to form a vagina.

The operation, in brief, consists of removing the penis and testes from their site, but keeping them attached to the body for the time being. This is most important. The perineum is then penetrated, and a new space created between the prostate and the bladder and rectum. The skin which was the penis is then inverted into this newly-created hole, and becomes the vagina. The remaining scrotal and genital tissue is then used to complete the vagina and create labia. This must be undertaken by a urologist, otherwise severe complications may result. Transsexuals' accounts of their operations are littered with horror stories about things that went terribly wrong. The urologist performing the operation has to know exactly where to locate the vagina, how deep to make the space, and how long he has got before penile and scrotal tissue dies and becomes useless.

Carried out privately, and depending on the surgeon, this sort of operation will cost £3,000 or more.

In Britain there are at the time of writing only two surgeons who are skilled enough to perform gender reassignment surgery of this second type – the only really satisfactory solution. There are several reasons for this, reasons which caused Jan Morris to become convinced that she must go to 'foreign parts beyond the law'. Most ethical surgeons are concerned only to save lives, and to perform only those operations which are necessary in this cause. They are not interested in mutilation. For a male surgeon the thought of removing healthy, functioning male organs is anathema. Furthermore there can never be any absolute guarantee that this particular operation will work. The male body, as the SHAFT handbook points out, was not designed to accommodate a female vagina, and so any attempt to make one will necessarily be less than perfect. Transsexuals can be very exacting and difficult to please, so any definition of success is likely to be subject to qualification.

There are, of course, legal considerations as well. In most European countries and in America no reputable surgeon will perform sex reassignment surgery without a written recommendation from a psychiatrist. One can begin to see why Casablanca has its attractions – no psychiatric assessment is needed, and Dr Georges Burou is considered to be one of the finest male-to-female transsexual surgeons in the world. The drawback for the surgeon is that if the patient later comes to regret the operation, he could charge the surgeon with assault. The risk of this is very small, but patients are becoming more litigious all the time, particularly in America. All these considerations mean that there is not exactly a rush among surgeons to perform this operation.

April Ashley's account of her operation describes how the surgery was followed by days of agonizing pain. Though some advances may have been made, it is unlikely, as she says, whether any significant improvements have taken place in the quarter-century since she changed over. The operation itself takes many hours to complete, and patients are not able to return to work for about two months afterwards. It is very major surgery indeed. Hormone treatment is usually stopped for a few weeks before and after, and strict attention to hygiene is needed while the labia and vagina heal up. The problem with creating an artificial vagina is the old one of nature abhorring a vacuum: the space keeps trying to close up. To prevent this, the passage has to be dilated regularly with a special instrument, a vaginal form, for 20 minutes twice a day.

For those with strong stomachs, April Ashley's book contains a vivid account of this unpleasant procedure:

Then came the first of what I shall call the horrors. At the end of the operation a speculum had been inserted into the vagina. This is a beak-like instrument which can be screwed open and closed. I called it my Oscar, after the film award. Later I christened it Donald Duck. It is needed to prevent the vagina from closing up and to guarantee the smooth healing of the vaginal walls which are heavily clotted with blood while the blood vessels realign themselves . . . Tablets cannot touch pain at this level.

Those awful nights . . . you lie there hot and soaking, you scream, you moan. You smell foul with clogged blood, you're bruised and swollen. And yet you are pitifully grateful too. Elated, completed at last, a relief so all-embracing that you imagine nothing will ever hurt you again. But these *petites operations* as Marie [the nurse] called them – I started to quake an hour before she arrived.

Even after two weeks, April Ashley could barely walk; she describes how her legs were 'ropes of jelly, and pains shot upward from thighs to chest'. Later, after leaving the clinic, she describes her first experiences of sex as a woman. For April, this was the culmination and almost the point of the exercise. It was also the proof of the operation's success. Other transsexuals say they are not particularly interested in physical sex.

One item which has to be used by immediate post-operative transsexuals is sanitary towels. Judy Cousins describes in her account how she had to wear them day and night until the bleeding and oozing stopped – so at least m-to-fs get some idea of what menstruation may be like. It's a little bit like the immediate post-natal stage of having a baby. The area continues to bleed for several weeks and post-operative patients are advised not to have sexual intercourse until it has completely healed up, say for two or three months.

Afterwards there is the more or less permanent problem of keeping the vaginal opening operational and large enough. Like any artificially created hole in the body, it will always try to close up. There are two ways of remedying this. One is to have regular sexual intercourse with a man. For some transsexuals, this is the most attractive solution. But as an increasing number of male-to-female transsexuals are now becoming radical lesbians, this is not always the answer. The other alternative is to keep dilating the area regularly with a special vaginal form.

Doctors usually point out to post-operative male-to-female transsexuals that the vagina may not be as functional or as able to afford sexual satisfaction as if it had been placed there by nature. As all women know, the vagina itself is virtually bereft of sensation anyway: it is the clitoris which responds to stimuli. Many post-operative transsexuals expect too much and can be disappointed when they do not get the orgasms they had fondly imagined would result after the operation.

After the all-important operation to remove male genitals and replace them with an approximation of female ones, many transsexuals decide to proceed with further operations. The most common are nose jobs and breast enlargement surgery. The decision as to whether or not to have a breast operation depends largely on how effective the female hormones have been at producing breasts.

While many male-to-female transsexuals have written their accounts and biographies, including detailed descriptions of their operations, we still await a similar account written by a female-to-male transsexual. They seem much more reticent about coming forward, identifying themselves and talking about what they have had done and why. For the moment, information is obtainable only from medical literature, which is itself very scanty.

Though surgery for male-to-female transsexuals can be carried out in one single operation, for female-to-male subjects there is a series of procedures which have to be carried out at different stages. Virtually all f-to-ms have a bilateral mastectomy and also a hysterectomy. These successfully remove the female organs. But the creation of an artificial penis is still very experimental and not completely satisfactory. Many patients decide not to go ahead with this operation.

The mastectomy operation is a fairly simple procedure and, if carried out sensitively, it is impossible afterwards to tell that female breasts have ever existed. One female-to-male transsexual said that he now had a fine white scar, but only he noticed it. The nipples are kept in place, though perhaps the areolae are somewhat larger than those of the average male. This is not normally noticeable, however.

The hysterectomy operation, usually performed at a later date as the ovaries and uterus are 'hidden' and therefore less of a worry, also brings considerable relief to f-to-ms. Though a hysterectomy is considered major surgery, it is a common enough procedure for biological women and should present no problems. A great many gynaecologists are competent to carry it out. In this operation, the bladder and vulva are left intact, and the patient will usually continue to urinate as before, that is, in the normal female fashion. Female-to-male transsexuals are usually advised to request that the hysterectomy is performed with a view of a later phalloplasty, leaving a vertical rather than a horizontal scar.

The first reasonably successful phalloplasty – as far as we are aware from the medical literature – was carried out on Michael (formerly Laura) Dillon, by Sir Harold Gillies, the famous wartime plastic surgeon, between 1945 and 1948. Since those days, techniques have advanced somewhat. A contemporary of Michael Dillon told me: 'He proudly showed me his penis. It was really primitive-looking – as if it had been hewn with an adze. The surgeon was making it up as he went along, and had nothing to guide him.' Dillon had about eleven operations in all before the artificial penis was completed. It was created by raising a pedicle – a tube of flesh – on the abdomen – and then grafting it into position, while realigning the urethra. Dillon's friend remembers: 'After the operation he was told, "Now pee." Of course he couldn't, and a tap had to be turned on so that in the end a tiny trickle emerged.'

There are still no standard techniques for the construction of a reasonably authentic-looking penis, or for the creation of natural-looking testes. There is an operation called scrotoplasty, whereby labia major are sewn together to form a kind of scrotum, and silicone implants are made. According to Green and Money, this artificial scrotum does not look very convincing. Most f-to-ms ask for phalloplasties simply to look normal, not so that they can then engage in sexual intercourse like a man. The 'fear of discovery' described by Green and Money is the main motivation for such an operation. There is currently no way of constructing an artificial penis from erectile tissue, though in some operations in America a stiffener can be inserted.

The tissue used to form a penis has to be attached to the urethra to make it completely leakproof and shrinkproof. As one can imagine, it is a very difficult and painful procedure, involving a series of deep skin grafts. The experiments in America with implant prostheses to make the penis capable of erecting have not been very satisfactory. The new penis will not be a sensitive organ like that of biological males, and is in fact virtually devoid of feeling. Mostly, however, the clitoris is left intact, so orgasm is possible.

The most complicated aspect of phalloplasty is construction of a male-type urethra, and there is always the risk of urinary infection afterwards. Many operations are needed before the artificial penis can be considered complete, and the whole procedure is fraught with danger and difficulty. Even so, most f-to-ms who have undergone phalloplasty feel pleased enough with the results. A reasonable approximation of the male organs of the desired sex is as much as they can hope for.

In Britain, all transsexuals are advised never to go for surgery until and unless they completely understand what is involved, and which procedures will be carried out. In America, the Harry Benjamin Foundation International Gender Dysphoria Association have prepared a list of 'standards of care' which they recommend should be followed by all doctors undertaking sex reassignment surgery. The document states that all surgeons carrying out such treatments should have proper professional qualifications and training, not just a certificate in sex therapy or counselling. The paper, which has been prepared for the medical profession, states that 'hormonal and surgical sex reassignment is extensive in its effects, is invasive to the integrity of the human body, has effects and consequences which are not, or not readily, reversible, and may be requested by persons experiencing short-term delusions or beliefs which may be later changed and reversed'. The document therefore recommends that persons seeking such treatment should be very carefully assessed over a period of time, and sets out the order in which surgical and hormonal treatments should be prescribed. The guidelines laid down in America for recommending treatment are:

(a) A sense of discomfort and inappropriateness about one's own anatomic sex.
(b) A wish to be rid of one's own genitals and to live as a member of the opposite sex.
(c) The disturbance has been continuous (not limited to periods of stress) for at least two years.
(d) There is no physical intersex or genetic abnormality.
(e) The condition is not due to another mental disorder, such as schizophrenia.

In other words, the conditions preceding sex reassignment must be carefully evaluated before any irreversible procedures are embarked upon. In countries where there if no national health service the patient has to pay for everything, of course, including the initial psychiatric counselling, but financial considerations will never stop a really determined patient.

The question that has to be asked at the end of the day is: is it all worth it? Are these unnatural and, from a physical point of view, completely unnecessary, invasive and cruelly painful operations justified by the outcome? Do patients noticeably achieve greater happiness as a result, and do they ever regret their self-imposed and self-sought mutilation?

In 1979 the famous Johns Hopkins Hospital in Baltimore stopped carrying out surgical sex reassignment when its staff came to the conclusion that sympathetic counselling could be just as successful. Janice Raymond, author of *The Transsexual Empire*, is also firmly of the belief that the right sort of non-stereotypical counselling is the right way forward. Her book contains an impassioned critique of surgical attempts at behaviour modification. She links it with lobotomies, clitoridectomies and other operations now largely seen as wicked.

But the Johns Hopkins decision, and Raymond's book, have not had any noticeable effect on the numbers of transsexuals seeking surgical treatment. Indeed, the indications are that surgery actually does work, however improbable it may seem that a surgical mutilation can cure a psychological condition. In late 1986 a survey was undertaken by Dr Charles Mate-Kole, a psychiatrist at the Charing Cross Hospital in London, where sex reassignment surgery has been pioneered. It seemed to confirm that, against all the odds, surgery did work. A group of male-to-female transsexuals were examined at different stages of their treatment. Questionnaires showed that those who had had no opeations but were still being assessed had extremely high levels of neurosis, while those who had completed treatment had very low scores on the same tests.

A total of 150 male-to-female transsexuals took part in the study. The various groups were assessed for obsessional neurosis, anxiety, phobic states, depression and hysteria. The highest neurotic symptoms of all were exhibited by those who had some time to go before their operation and had only just undertaken the decision to seek treatment. The lowest scores were obtained by post-operative transsexuals, and it seemed that the more time had elapsed since the operation, the more peaceful, relaxed and unstressed they became. Though surgery is fraught with difficulties, pain and disappointments, it pales into insignificance compared with the agony of having to continue living in the 'wrong' sex. All transsexuals accept that their surgery is only cosmetic and can never make them into biological opposites, but this doesn't seem to matter too much.

In the early days, it is possible that many people who sought treatment were highly disturbed, and perhaps more in need of psychiatric treatment than surgery. Nowadays, unless the intending transsexual goes straight to Casablanca, the long process of psychiatric prior assessment must be undergone, and this should in theory ensure that only those who are fully prepared for the risks and consequences reach the operating table.

How far transsexual assessment, as carried out at gender-identity clinics, contributes to the continuation of outdated sex stereotyping is another matter. In an ideal world, perhaps, no one would bother too much what body-shape or sex others happened to have – the mind and the spirit would be the important things. We should be able to transcend body-shapes and assess people purely on their personalities, interests and characters. In reality, an individual's experiences and outlook are intimately determined and influenced by body-shape and gender. There seems, at the current time, to be an absolute distinction between men and women, which makes the gap between the sexes very wide although some people believe that it is less wide than it was 30 years ago. Nobody, however, could seriously believe that the sexes have come together in such a way that we see people as human beings first, and men or women second. Therefore, until our attitudes change drastically, it seems that transsexual surgery will continue to be the answer for those who are gender-dysphoric. Certainly, the many transsexuals whose comments and opinions have contributed to this present book have no doubts about the matter. They are utterly convinced that surgery and hormones have, quite literally, saved their lives. Pre-operative transsexuals are very often in a sorry state indeed, and improve out of all recognition once their treatment has been completed. They feel they can then take their place in the world as normal people. Their outward physical appearance conforms at last to their sense of personal identity. Once they can live without the fear of discovery, which all pre-operative transsexuals endure, a great burden of worry just falls away.

CHAPTER 4

Transsexuals and the law

Transsexuals, particularly after they have had their operations, find themselves in an anomalous legal situation. For some purposes they have to remain in their original sex, while for others they are considered fully operational members of their new sex.

Although surgically transformed transsexuals have been in existence for nearly 40 years, the law remains ambivalent about them. It used to be the case in Britain that birth certificates could be amended following sex-change surgery, but since the Corbett v. Corbett (April Ashley) case in 1970, British law has stated that the original, chromosomal sex must remain, even though all the outward organs and physical accoutrements of that sex have now disappeared. This means that transsexuals cannot remarry in their new sex, and that on every occasion for which they have to produce their birth certificates their secret will be out.

Over the years, authorities have relaxed the rules for other documents, allowing driving licences, bank cards, passports and insurance cards to be altered. But the law remains unchanged on retirement matters. The present situation in Britain is such that a post-operative transsexual has to retire from work as if still a member of the original sex, and becomes eligible for a state pension on the grounds of his/her biological sex. Ferocious and prolonged campaigns by transsexuals to get the law changed have not so far been successful even though the matter has been taken to the European court in Strasbourg.

As the April Ashley case permanently altered the law concerning transsexuals, I shall here briefly describe it. Some years after her operation April Ashley, formerly merchant seaman George Jamieson, married the Honourable Arthur Cameron Corbett, son of Lord Rowallan, the Chief Scout. At the time she was 26 and he was 42. The marriage didn't work out and in time the odd couple decided to divorce. It was an astonishingly messy affair. In 1967 Corbett filed a divorce petition to the effect that the marriage was 'null and void and of no effect because the respondent at the time of the ceremony was a person of the male sex, or in the alternative for a decree of nullity on the ground that the marriage was never consummated owing to the incapacity or wilful refusal of the respondent to consummate it.' April Ashley countered by seeking a similar decree of nullity. Corbett's contention was that as April Ashley was a biological male, the marriage had never and could never really have taken place.

April's argument was that, since the operation, she had been functioning and living as a female and, indeed, could not possibly function any longer as a man. The case was held in the days before the divorce laws were relaxed, and when one or other party had to have 'grounds'. Accordingly, all kinds of expert witnesses – doctors and psychiatrists from all possible persuasions – were called, to testify whether or not April Ashley was still a man. If she was, then the marriage simply never took place, as two people of the same sex cannot legally be married to each other. The whole outcome of the case hinged on the definition of male and female, and to which sex April Ashley could be considered to belong. Gynaecologists performed the so-called three-finger test, which consisted of putting three fingers into the vagina to see whether it could accommodate a normal-sized penis. April Ashley writes in her 'odyssey' that she passed that one.

In the end, however, experts and judges decided that as April Ashley had been born a male she still *was* a male, whatever operations had been carried out subsequently. Once a male always a male was their final verdict, and no amount of cosmetic surgery or hormone treatment could ever alter this basic fact. Doctors found that April Ashley's chromosomal sex was XY: of this there was no possible doubt, but confusion remained over gonadal and psychological sex. Extensive tests were applied.

Mr Justice Ormrod, who presided over the case, held

that the respondent was not, and had not been, a woman at the time of the marriage and that the marriage was accordingly void. This verdict meant that henceforth in Britain, though all other documents may be changed to the new name and sex, the most important one of all, the birth certificate, must remain unaltered, except where, for some medical reason, sex has been wrongly assigned at birth.

For all practical purposes, therefore, April Ashley – and all subsequent transsexuals – could be considered female, but the true, the original sex could never be altered. On hearing the judgement many transsexuals' hearts sank. Large numbers of them maintained that their marriages, legally and properly conducted, confirmed that they really had 'changed sex'. Yet, from a medical and biological point of view, post-operative transsexuals cannot genuinely be considered to have changed sex. Nowadays, they have to accept this before treatment can be started. Few would argue about this, as it is a medical fact. In her book Janice Raymond coined the expression male-to-constructed-female (and *vice versa*) to describe post-operative transsexuals, and at least one, Rachael Webb, always refers to herself in this way.

But, though the biology may be clear, the legal position remains muddy and unresolved. No doubt the birth certificate ruling is intended to stop people passing themselves off as somebody else – a fear which is virtually groundless, as the great majority of transsexuals simply want to be acceptable, as completely as possible, in their new sex. There is no evidence that any would wish to exploit a relaxation of the ruling for criminal purposes. Nor can transsexuals be considered insane: if they were, they would simply not get through the stringent psychological tests which precede treatment.

The April Ashley case defined maleness and femaleness as an individual's aptitude to conceive or beget children. It was the ability to *marry* and function as a natural member of the desired sex which decided the case in the end. Of course, the judgement raised all kinds of considerations as to what a 'real' marriage might be. If a woman is past the age of reproduction, may she not contract a legal marriage? If she has had a hysterectomy, is her marriage no longer legal? If a man is paralysed and confined to a wheelchair, unable to have sexual intercourse, may he not legally marry? Is marriage basically a biological or a cultural institution? The questions thrown up by the Corbett case resound still, but the outcome was that a post-operative transsexual may not marry at all, in either the original or the new sex.

Now that formal marriages are not so much part of the apparatus for qualifying as an acceptable member of society, the question is perhaps of less interest than it was. Many post-operative transsexuals are living happily with permanent partners to whom they consider themselves married. But the fact remains that they can never walk up the aisle. A comparatively recent case, which received television coverage, concerned a post-operative transsexual who was about to marry, as a woman. It led to a *Jane Eyre*-type situation with somebody shouting out, 'This marriage cannot take place'. The 'bride' was a biological male and accordingly, the marriage did not take place. But the couple lived together for sixteen years anyway, as man and wife.

As British law stands, if any such marriage were to be conducted, the transsexual would technically be committing perjury; he or she would be open to a charge of misleading a public registrar and if charged could be convicted under the Perjury Act of 1911.

Of course, before any sex reassignment treatment is started, the pre-operative transsexual has to be single. This means that all intending transsexuals must normally, if married, get divorced as a first step. Jan Morris describes the impact the 'be single' edict had on her attitude to psychiatrists and doctors in London:

I had long been assured by my London doctors that when the time came, there would be no difficulty. But when, in the spring of 1972, I felt myself ready for the last hurdle, and my family too, I discovered an unexpected snag. The surgeon who had interviewed me and who accepted me for surgery at the Charing Cross hospital, declined to operate until Elizabeth and I were divorced. I saw his point, for he could not know the nature of the relationship between us, and indeed I recognized that we must be divorced in the end. But after a lifetime of fighting battles, I did not feel in a mood to offer my destiny like a sacrifice upon the benches of Her Majesty's Judges. Who knew what degradations we might both endure? What business was it of theirs anyway?

By this time Jan Morris' day-to-day documents had already been altered. She had taken a new first name by statutory declaration, and had her bank statements changed from Mr to Miss. She had received a new driving licence and a new passport without any trouble at all. She was by now living openly as a woman, though as yet she had not undergone the operation.

In order to avoid a messy, humiliating divorce – perhaps not wishing to face a similar process to that undergone by April Ashley – Jan Morris took herself off to foreign parts 'beyond the law' to achieve her surgical transformation.

For most transsexuals, the first thing on the road to a permanent change-over is a change of name. This can be done quite simply by statutory declaration at a local solicitor's. The great majority of transsexuals change only their first names and keep their original surnames. Some, however, like Judy Cousins and April Ashley, decide to change both. It depends to what extent a complete change of identity is required, or how much the privacy of relatives needs to be protected, should there be subsequent publicity. A statutory declaration is a perfectly legal document, and once the name has been changed it then becomes possible to alter all documentation. The national insurance card can be changed without any difficulty, as can income tax records, medical and driving licences and bank cards. With the passport, the situation is slightly more complicated. Before the actual operation takes place, it is possible to change only the name and not the gender. So a pre-operative passport would read 'John Smith' or 'Jane Smith', leaving out the Mr, Mrs or Ms.

SHAFT comments in its handbook that the list of record changes can seem endless for it includes mortgage, gas, electricity and telephone accounts, water rates, Land Registry entries and insurance policies as well as those already mentioned. Transsexuals attending gender-identity clinics can get help with altering their documents. It is even possible, according to SHAFT, to get GCE, CSE or degree certificates changed to the new name. Of course, as SHAFT points out, no records that have already been published may be altered, such as armed forces records. Those who wish to keep their post-operative identity a secret from the world at large are usually advised to change their last name as well as the first, and make a completely new start in life. Such a change of name doesn't raise any overwhelming legal problems.

It is not an offence as such for a man or woman to appear in public dressed in the clothes of the opposite sex, but police have sometimes charged transvestites and pre-operative transsexuals with 'insulting behaviour' when they use ladies' loos. To avoid any possibility of this, it is possible to obtain from the gender-identity clinic an authorization document, stating that the person carrying the certificate is currently undergoing sex reassignment treatment. Most often, the proof that an individual is having medical treatment and suffers from a 'condition' will protect him or her from trouble.

As a post-operative male-to-female transsexual remains ultimately male in the eyes of the law, she cannot, as far as the courts are concerned, be raped. If she were to be attacked in such a way, she would therefore not be able to bring a rape charge, only one of indecent assault. Bringing a case of this nature would always result in the transsexual's case history being fully explained in court, so transsexuals are usually advised to be very careful about bringing charges.

Certain sections of the legal profession still regard transsexuals as subversive and potentially dangerous people, so their position is very shaky in comparison with that of most others. If a transsexual were to commit a crime which could result in his/her being sent to prison, an already difficult situation would be compounded: as British law (and that of many other countries) stands, a post-operative transsexual would be sent to the prison appropriate to his/her original gender, rather than the newly-established one, and at the same time hormone treatment could well be discontinued – at the discretion of the prison doctors.

In the old days, many male-to-female transsexuals hoped that a Prince Charming might suddenly appear and carry them off to a life of luxury and ease. At that time it seems likely that most biological men had a completely unrealistic idea of what it was like to be a woman. In any case, the Prince Charming fantasy would always turn out to be just that – fantasy – and by far the great majority of transsexuals had to continue to earn a living and be self-supporting, as they do today. Some discover that they cannot find employment and are reduced to living on welfare, but all have to assume that they will continue in employment. Indeed, most prefer to, as the majority are professional people who would not be happy to live in idleness. However, from a work point of view, their position does pose problems.

Although birth certificates rarely have to be produced and the courts have stated that they are to be regarded as a historical fact rather than 'evidence' of any kind, the fact remains that anybody can be asked to show a birth certificate as a condition of employment. The potential employer has every right to request this, and even to insist on it, particularly if the employee is joining a pension scheme or superannuation benefits are being calculated. The employee may not withhold documentary proof of his/her birth date and it may therefore become impossible for a transsexual to keep his/her past a secret from a new firm, unless a passport bearing the new name and sex designation is provided instead.

One court case, White *v.* the British Sugar Corporation, illustrated what a damning document the birth certificate can be. Here the claimant, a female-to-male transsexual, was refused a job already offered when he was discovered to be a transsexual. The case went to an industrial tribunal, which ruled that the claimant was 'really' a woman and that therefore there had been no discrimination under existing laws. The Sex Discrimination Act of 1975 does not apply to transsexuals. Even though they often consider themselves discriminated against, there is little in law that they can do about it.

With regard to unemployment benefit, the position is exactly the same as for any other unemployed person, man or woman. When it comes to the peculiar 'cohabiting' law, whereby a woman may have her social security benefit stopped if she is known to be living with a man, difficulties may be encountered. At least one male-to-female transsexual has had her benefit stopped when she was found to be living with a man, but this decision was reversed on appeal. The DHSS may try to argue that the original sexual assignment is the correct one for assessing benefit. The whole situation is confused, and cannot change until new definitions of men and women are introduced: either that, or the law will in future not have to stop making the gender of a person – either orginal or reassigned – a decisive factor in the outcome of particular legal issues. The present confusion regarding transsexuals has arisen largely because men and women are treated differently under the law. If they were treated exactly the same, many current anomalies would vanish. The non-sense that prevails not just in law but in many other areas of life has prompted writers such as Janice Raymond to bemoan the sex stereotyping and polarization of the sexes in today's society.

Although the verdict of the April Ashley case was that transsexuals may not marry, it allowed that for all other purposes – work, insurance, travel and so on, the new status was completely legal and valid. So any DHSS official who tries to tell a post-operative transsexual that he or she is not a 'real' man or woman is actually breaking the law.

The position regarding retirement pensions remains anomalous, and upsets many transsexuals. Again, it underlines how differently men and women are regarded in our society. When Judy Cousins was 60, she applied for a retirement pension and was refused because she was 'really' a man, and would therefore have to wait until she was 65. She appealed against this decision, but the pension-fund administrators were adamant and she had to wait. At the time of writing it looks as though the law on retirement ages may soon be changed, however. Private pension schemes do not follow the state's ruling in this respect, and usually even the pre-operative transsexual may be treated as a member of the acquired gender, so long as he or she is armed with the all-important piece of paper from the gender-identity clinic.

It is still the case that the transsexual identity must be revealed on any life assurance application and in the event of the death of the insured the insurance company would have to see the birth certificate, which would of course reveal the original sex.

Some insurance companies will insure the life of a pre-operative transsexual intending to undergo reassignment surgery, at an increased premium. At the time of writing, Lloyds will issue a short-term life insurance at about £25 per £1000 of cover for the cost of the reassignment surgery, plus four months' convalescence afterwards, provided the person insured is aged about 30 years. Wills and questions of inheritance are unaffected, once identity has been proved. Most transsexuals, of course, do not have titles or important pieces of property to bequeath, but where such are a factor ranks are very quickly closed.

One wonders whether April Ashley's case would have gone quite so catastrophically against her had she not been George Jamieson from a Liverpool slum, and had her husband not been a member of the landed aristocracy, and the eldest son. Something rather similar happened in the case of Michael Dillon, who, if he could have fathered a son, would have stood to inherit a baronetcy. Only one newspaper story ever came out about Michael Dillon, and this concerned the inheritance and baronetcy. It seems as if, in British law at least, transsexual status becomes very questionable when there is money or property at stake. In the April Ashley case, if the marriage had not been declared null and void, April might have had some claim on her husband's inheritance. As it was, she was considered never to have been his wife in the first place. Although Michael Dillon's birth certificate, two decades before the April Ashley decision, had been altered, his status as a man was still in question.

SHAFT feels that the present laws regarding transsexuals are nothing short of absurd, as they give with one

hand what they take away with the other. Initial determination of sex, it claims, is usually based on the most
cursory of examinations, and yet the ramifications of the
conclusion drawn last a lifetime. But of course, though the
initial examination of a newborn baby may only take a
second, it is unlikely that a more lengthy procedure at this
stage would achieve anything. Transsexuals are *not* biological members of their chosen sex, and never can be.
Despite the fact that the change may be very successful,
the ultimate indicator of gender must remain the chromosomal test. The real question must be: is it right to treat
men and women differently under the law? Is there any
real reason why legally binding marriages should not be
conducted between people of the same sex? The old
prayer-book idea that marriage was ordained for the sake
of being fruitful and multiplying seems as out of date as
horse-drawn carriages. Are couples who do not wish for
and do not intend to have children legally married? Are
couples who are infertile legally married? Are couples
who marry late, beyond their reproductive years, to be
considered not legally married?

An overhaul of the present legislature is desperately
overdue. The current legal attitude to transsexuals, whereby nobody is quite sure whether they should be treated as
a member of their original or their chosen sex, points up
the absurdities. As April Ashley says in her book, if she
couldn't function as a woman, she certainly couldn't
perform as a man. Would she, then, and people like her,
be legally allowed to marry in the *original* sex, after the
operation?

From time to time dissatisfied transsexuals make
attempts to get the law changed in their favour. The latest
case to come before the European Court was that of Mark
Rees, which was comprehensively reported in the British
press during 1986. Mark Rees, formerly Brenda, felt that
the present law regarding the unalterability of the birth
certificate was antiquated nonsense and took his case to
court. For a long time it looked as though he might win,
but in the end, on 17 October 1986, his appeal was
rejected by the European Court in Strasbourg. Rees, in his
early forties, had hoped that he might win, both for

himself and for his fellow transsexuals, the right to have the birth certificate changed.

No such luck.

His lawyer, Nicholas Blake, commented thus on the outcome:

The judgement is a considerable disappointment not only for transsexuals but also to all those who hoped the court would be prepared to be more 'activist' and set standards for member states to follow, rather than themselves to defer to existing practices. The court appears to have accepted the Government's argument that the UK does not recognize the applicant's sexual identity for a variety of purposes. The court notes that passports, driving licences and national insurance certificates are all issued in the names reflecting the male identity of Mark Rees. But as there is no system of civil status certificates in the UK, and the law freely permits an individual to change a name, these practices merely reflect that these documents are documents of description and not of legal identity.

As in the April Ashley case, ultimately it came down to a question of marriageability. The judges were unanimous: 15–0 on the marriage question, and voted 12–3 against the birth certificate issue. So the verdict was overwhelmingly against transsexuals.

The birth certificate situation is not uniform throughout the world. In Austria, Ireland and Great Britain, they cannot be altered but in Portugal, Spain and Italy ways have been found of amending the original document to give legal status in the acquired gender.

In America, where most of the research into transsexuality has been carried out, the situation remains complicated. A few states will willingly issue new birth certificates, without fuss, whereas others require a court order before *any* documents, including passport and driving licence, can be changed. Otherwise, the American definition of gender remains identical to that used by the British and European gender-identity clinics: that original biological sex can never be changed, and that gonadal and genital sex is never basically altered either; the changes made can only be considered cosmetic. The famous Casablanca surgeon Georges Burou, who has carried out conversions on more than 800 transsexuals, has no illusions about what he is doing. He said once: 'I don't change men into women. I transform male genitals into genitals that have a female aspect. All the rest is in the patient's mind.'

Endocrinal or hormonal sex can, given modern drugs, be transformed radically and it seems that, for practical purposes, the law does go along with a change of sex. 'It is legally possible,' says Janice Raymond, 'to change sex. However, the whole area of *legal* sex has been one of contention for the transsexual who wishes to have sex-conversion surgery validated.'

It seems more than likely that, before long, the law will have to change to favour transsexuals, partly because there are now so many of them, and partly because our former definitions of male and female were largely governed by women being regarded as legally inferior to men. Before the present law regarding birth certificates can be altered, there has to be some radical thinking about our present sex stereotyping and about what actually designates people male or female – or, indeed, whether it should matter very much to anybody except the individuals in question which they are. With regard to the outcome of the Mark Rees case, SHAFT commented in one of its newsletters:

It has been said that the European court represents the lowest common denominator of the consciousness of middle-class Europe. There was obviously a gut reaction that marriage involving a transsexual was somehow sacreligious or anarchic. That they [the European court] should then try to rationalize this by claiming that marriage is only to do with biological sex and procreation shows an incredible ostrich-like reaction that ignores the reality of the situation and reflects no credit on them.

Mark Rees has said that he intends to carry on fighting, and is undaunted by the Strasbourg decision. It will take more – perhaps many more – cases before the present law is reversed or amended, and possibly some dramatic incident, like the April Ashley case, to do it. The current laws concerning transsexuals reflect that judges and legislators do not really know what to think, but remain vaguely uneasy about the phenomenon of transsexuality. They perhaps wish it didn't exist or that, if it did, transsexuals would oblige by never appearing in public and never making the slightest nuisance of themselves. Transsexuals themselves feel that the laws will only change in their favour once they are generally accepted to be normal, intelligent, rational human beings rather than kinky curiosities.

CHAPTER 5

How transsexuality affects others

The most difficult decision a pre-operative transsexual has to make is whether or not to go ahead with an irreversible mutilating series of surgical procedures. Having made that decision, or rather, having found life so completely untenable in the original gender that not having surgery can hardly be considered a viable option, the question then arises of how best to go about it with as little disruption and upset as possible. As changing sex involves an almost complete change of identity, many transsexuals agonize over whether to tell people, when to tell and how to tell them, and how to lead a reasonably satisfying and positive life after the surgeon's work has been completed.

In the old days, the commonest solution was simply to lie low for a bit, then emerge at some time in the future with a new name, a new set of records and a new persona which, with any luck, would provide very few clues to the former identity. In order to achieve this, pioneering transsexuals often felt they had no choice but to undergo a complete name change, first name and surname, then move to another part of the country, or even to another country. Very often, this was done mainly to spare relatives and spouses the pain of knowing that a gender change had been undertaken. Many transsexuals felt, usually with justification, that their families would simply not be able to accept them in a different sex.

This was Judy Cousins' solution. When, at the age of 53, and with most of her family responsibilities now over, she finally decided to change over, she arranged to 'disappear' so that her family would not be able to find her. She felt this was the kindest and most compassionate way of achieving her aim, and one that would spare her family the anguish of knowing the truth. In the event, she found it was more difficult to disappear than she had imagined, and she was eventually traced. Newspaper stories appeared about her, and so in the end her family had to know. After her change-over, she arranged to meet her family. Her grown-up daughters have been able to accept the change, but her former wife and son have not. Judy's younger daughter Penny is particularly unfazed by it all. 'After all,' she reflected when I interviewed her, 'I had a real father for the first twelve years of my life, when it mattered. Now I introduce Judy or describe her to my friends as my father, who has had a sex-change. Nobody bothers about it in the least.'

Now that transsexualism is becoming more accepted in everyday society, the more modern solution is to come clean at the earliest possible opportunity, to explain to the family what is happening, even if they don't understand, and put them in the picture. Once this is done, most transsexuals try to live their lives pretty much as before, keeping the same job if possible and trying to continue in a good relationship with their former spouses. Some do manage to remain close and affectionate, but this must be considered a bonus, not to be expected as of right. Very many spouses simply do not understand, and become horrified when they are told.

In Britain the present method of sex reassignment insists that transsexuals must be divorced before any treatment can be started. Accordingly, Jan Morris was divorced from her wife Elizabeth before hers began, but, as she tells us in *Conundrum*, they have remained close friends. Jan Morris is also on good terms with her four children.

Another couple, Rae and Isabel Smith, who told their story to *The Star*, the London daily newspaper, are happily living together as 'sisters'. Rae Smith, formerly Raymond, was thought to be born with Klinefelter's Syndrome, whereby a genetic male has an extra X chromosome which means that certain female characteristics may appear. At any rate, he was born with deformed genitals and doctors couldn't quite tell which sex he was meant to be. He was designated male, and later had a series of operations, but always there was a degree of intersexuality.

As Raymond Smith had fathered three children, he must have been basically male. In the newspaper story, Rae described to reporter Robert Coole how, after his marriage to Isabel (it was a second marriage for both of them), he decided one day that he was really a woman, and that it was time to make the change-over. This was all discussed with Isabel before any treatment was begun, and today they live together as two women.

Other male-to-female transsexuals are also continuing to live with their original partners, in a sisterly relationship, though all say the partnership has had to undergo profound transformation, with considerable adjustment on the part of the spouse.

In my researches for this book, I have not come across any female-to-male transsexual who was married in the original sex. They must, presumably, exist, but if so, they are keeping themselves very quiet indeed. Nor have I located any female-to-male transsexual who became a mother before the change-over. Most usually these people see themselves as rather 'butch', and the thought of getting married and having a family is utterly repugnant to them. They regard the prospect of sexual intercourse with a man not just as distasteful, but as completely impossible. Their problems tend to centre on exactly how to break the news to their parents, as the decision to change over is commonly made while they are teenagers or in their early twenties.

The average male-to-female transsexual, by contrast, is normally not noticeably effeminate or homosexual, and more often than not will marry (before the change is made), partly to try to convince himself that he is as masculine as the next man. Melanie Martin, a male-to-female transsexual, told me: 'I can remember thinking as I walked down the aisle and met my bride at the altar: I've done it, I've proved I'm normal.' Of course, that marriage didn't last: Melanie's sense of being female grew stronger, rather than weaker, during the years of the marriage. Many male-to-female transsexuals erroneously believe that marriage will effectively kill their long-held wish to be women. In fact, it usually has just the opposite effect, as they are in daily contact with a woman and have ready access to a wardrobe full of women's clothes.

Sometimes the urge to cross-dress becomes irresistible. Many former wives of transsexuals have described how they became aware of their husband's strange fetish. Very often they are frightened by it, as well as dismayed and shocked. They know that it isn't normal, but hope that somehow the condition can be treated and cured. Many wives simply never recover from the shock of seeing the man they married in good faith, thinking he was a perfectly average male, dressed in female clothes. They recoil. Some never want to see their husbands again.

It is not uncommon for wives, on discovering that their husbands wish to change sex and live as a woman, to deny them access to the children and to the family home, and simply refuse to discuss the matter. (By far the great majority of male-to-female transsexuals have become fathers, with the attendant family responsibilities, long before the decision to change over is finally taken.)

Is there a 'best' way of managing the situation? Can a transsexual seriously hope to continue much as before, or is it advisable to change identity as completely as possible, move elsewhere, and take a new type of job as well as a new location?

Rachael Webb, well-known for her left-wing views, and a Labour councillor in Brixton, used to be a long-distance lorry-driver. On making the decision to change over, however, she could no longer do this job, which she loved, so she qualified as a shorthand typist and word-processor operator. Now she is a community worker. She moved to central London, having previously lived on the east coast of England, and took on a completely new identity as a radical lesbian feminist. But as a member of the Labour Party and campaigner for gay and lesbian rights she laid herself open to a smear campaign by the Tory press. The news that she had had a sex-change operation 'on the rates' became known to all. Similarly, Judy Cousins' whereabouts and continuing existence – after she had carefully staged a mock suicide – became known through a newspaper report. Transsexuals continue to remain prime newspaper fodder, and those who do not wish to attract any publicity to themselves must be very careful about their actions. Unlooked-for publicity can make life very difficult, as many have discovered to their cost.

Nowadays, when most pre-operative transsexuals – at least if they are seeking treatment at an NHS hospital – have first to attend gender-identity clinics, where the considerations of re-entering society in the new rôle are all carefully evaluated, the pre-operative patient may find that he or she has to go along a path already mapped out by the clinic, otherwise treatment might be refused. This usually means continuing in the same job, armed with the essential certificate.

Workmates then have to observe the strange spectacle of a colleague gradually changing sex before their eyes. One female-to-male transsexual described this:

I left work on Christmas Eve as a woman and returned after New Year as a man, wearing men's suits and using the men's toilets. Of course, the hormones don't work immediately, and it was several months before I began to look like a man. At first I was an extremely feminine-looking man, and got more obviously masculine as the months went by.

The solution that April Ashley adopted, a quarter of a century ago, was to become a drag artist in Paris nightclubs, while still male, though dressing and acting fulltime as a woman. April Ashley was lucky in that she had no family responsibilities at all, and no 'position' to keep up in the outside world. A large proportion of transsexuals are, however, professionally qualified people with jobs that carry considerable responsibility. Many now find that there is surprisingly little difficulty involved in keeping their jobs, particularly if they are lecturers or teachers. The civil service, too, has been amazingly tolerant, given its rather stuffy image, about accepting transsexuals.

Transsexual surgery is not normally available to those under the age of 21, even though the age of majority is now considered to be 18. Although from a cosmetic point of view the younger the transsexual the better the end result, the fact is that many young people find it hard to cope with their duality, and may take some time to make up their minds finally to change over, With age comes increasing confidence, as well as an increasing conviction that a change-over at some stage is essential to happiness and sanity.

Most parents find it hard – perhaps impossible – to accept that their son or daughter is 'really' the opposite sex to that stated on the birth certificate and hope – usually in vain – that their offspring will 'grow out of it'. Such hopes are almost always groundless, and the fact is that most teenage transsexuals get very little, if any, help, from any source at all. With no parental support, they often become even more difficult and rebellious than the average teenager. Suicide attempts and disappearances are also common. The sympathetic parent who understands something of transsexualism can sometimes come to terms with it, and there is on record at least one instance of a gender rôle change being permitted at school. Many young transsexuals, feeling alienated from a hostile world, try to obtain surgery as soon as possible, before undergoing the recommended psychiatric assessment. This can prove to be a bad mistake; more than one young male-to-female transsexual has not been happy in the new female rôle and has tried to change back.

Life is perhaps most difficult of all for the married transsexual with a young family. Clearly a drastic break has to be made with the former lifestyle, but how can this be done smoothly? Most GICs recommend that the pre-operative transsexual should discuss the implications of the situation frankly and simply with all those who have to know about it. Even if they do not fully understand, it can make things easier in the future. All transsexuals who have made their private decision to go ahead must accept that, from now on, they may be entirely on their own, and may well find their former life in permanent shreds. Some spouses may be encouraging and accepting, but this cannot be guaranteed or expected.

Transsexuals should consider themselves particularly fortunate if they can hang on to their jobs and also continue in close personal relationships begun before the change-over. The usual advice given is that it is unfair to conceal from your spouse the fact that you have begun hormone therapy, though the spouse's permission is not needed for this.

The most vexing question for transsexuals usually concerns children. Most of those who are parents would love to continue to have a close relationship with their children. But how do children themselves cope with having a transsexual parent? All the available evidence seems to suggest that most are not unduly disturbed, and certainly there has been no documented example of a child following suit – that is, wishing to change sex in order to copy the parent.

Most psychiatrists and social workers advise that where there are very young children, it is better for them not to be told until after puberty. This of course presents enormous difficulties for the parent who wishes to continue living in the same house and continue in the same lifestyle. Studies carried out in America suggest that children are not adversely affected by a parent's transsexuality, and can usually cope remarkably well with this information. One doctor who regularly handles transsexual problems stated: 'In terms of children, my own experience has been that there have not been any significant or profound psychological aberrations in children whose parents have undergone gender reorientation.' Most often it is the other adults who have the problems.

Where there are young children, the question of access may cause friction. All divorced fathers with young families have to face this, but the matter becomes even more difficult to resolve when the father is a transsexual. In the eyes of some lawyers, such a parent has completely abdicated responsibility by changing sex and can no longer expect any sympathy from the law. In 1981, an appeal court in Britain granted restricted access to a male parent who had changed sex. Access is more likely to be granted, it seems, if the parent has not disappeared during the change-over but has kept up regular contact throughout.

In its latest handbook, SHAFT offers some guidelines to transsexual parents who may have to go to court and fight for access over children. Do not expect, warns the handbook, to be treated exactly the same as any other father fighting for access to his children.

In reality, the law is traditional, conventional and has an abhorrence of anything it perceives as abnormal or irrational. It is certainly a decade or so behind the medical profession and even public opinion. So forget pipe dreams like custody (even joint), care and control, or even staying access. No matter how bad a parent you perceive your partner to be, she is likely to be viewed by the court as infinitely preferable to a transsexual parent.

SHAFT advises obtaining the best legal advice possible, as early as possible, and bearing in mind that transsexual problems need a particular kind of legal skill. It may also be necessary to get psychiatric reports in advance, as the courts may well order these, if they are not already available. The psychiatrist should see the children, too, preferably together with the parent, in order to be able to judge the quality of the relationship.

It is unlikely, according to SHAFT, that access, if granted, will be anything other than severely restricted, so all intending transsexuals should brace themselves for the possibility that the operation may mean the effective end of any proper relationship with their children. For many, this is the hardest thing of all to accept but, even so, it does not usually deter transsexuals from going ahead.

Apart from work, marital and family considerations, the other important aspect is how to 'pass' successfully as a member of the other sex. Here, both GICs and SHAFT have been accused of needless sex stereotyping, of trying to pigeonhole people into preconceived and artificial modes of behaviour. There is certainly a strong tendency, in the newly-created female, of overdoing feminine gestures, make-up and dress, and to look more like a man in drag than a real woman.

'The problem,' says SHAFT, 'is not simply one of passing in physical appearance and voice but also in manner, vocabulary and personality; not merely passing, but *being*. It is necessary for the transsexual to be successful as a person, and not merely as an actor . . . To pursue a certain lifestyle at the cost of alienating all normal social contacts, and quite possibly being jobless, is hardly a recipe for future happiness. There is little social discrimination against successful transsexuals, because they are not distinguishable from any others of their new sex, but for those unfortunate enough to have made an unconvincing transformation, life can be terribly hard.'

Very few transsexuals, it must be said, achieve a completely smooth transformation into the new sex, and the longer they have been living in the original one, the harder it all becomes. Inevitably, in the original rôle, masculine and feminine types of behaviour are picked up, simply because one is living in that identity and is treated as such. Male-to-female transsexuals have to worry about their hair, clothes, gestures, and so on. Jan Morris, who lived a very masculine life prior to her change-over, said that a couple of bracelets on the wrist were enough to convince most people that she was female rather than male. They were sufficient to tip her into being unquestionably accepted as a woman. She – like all of the more intelligent transsexuals – has not found it necessary to go in for long blonde wings, bright red lipstick and noticeably glamorous outfits.

Marion Coughlin, a social worker at the Charing Cross Hospital who helps transsexuals to come to terms with the social aspects of the change-over, has observed:

The majority of the young ones look quite feminine when they first come in. But many completely overdo the feminine clothes and wear high heels and lots of make-up. They have an image of a woman which is often quite unrealistic. Most of the ones I see don't look at all like Jan Morris. My job is to organize grooming classes, beauty therapists and so on. We also recommend that the male-to-female transsexuals attend speech therapy classes, which are run by Adult Education Centres.

The beauty therapist attached to Charing Cross Hospital, where the majority of transsexuals go for assessment, will look at each individual and suggest how the appearance can be improved while remaining as convincing as possible. Marion Coughlin said: 'Many look bizarre at first, but they come out of it in time. It often takes two years to adjust completely to a new rôle.'

Obviously a certain amount of consideration has to be given to behaviour, but most transsexuals discover that, so long as they look normal, they can just be themselves and nobody will raise an eyebrow. There is no need to pretend to be excessively feminine and silly, like Marilyn Monroe in *Some Like It Hot*, or to pretend a sudden interest in cricket scores or electronics, if a female-to-male. Transsexuals of both persuasions are advised that their problems will not magically disappear after surgery. Most do, however, discover that life gets steadily better as they ease into the new rôle, which feels far more comfortable and right than the old one.

Post-operatively, all transsexuals will eventually be confronted with the dilemma of whom to tell. The usual advice given is not to tell anybody who does not absolutely have to know, unless you intend writing a book, or appearing on television and describing your experiences to the world. Some post-operative transsexuals feel nervous of mixing with ordinary people and try to belong to a ghetto of like-minded individuals. Most have found that this doesn't work. The best course of action seems to be to go out into the real world and mix with ordinary people, however difficult this may be thought at first. The whole object of the exercise – psychiatric assessment, hormone treatment and surgery – is after all to make people feel more, rather than less, normal. SHAFT particularly advises against forming any close emotional liaisons with the now-opposite sex while still at the pre-operative stage. Their collective experience has shown that relationships formed at the in-between stage rarely last, and can cause even more pain and upset.

Several transsexuals who have managed their change-over without undue disruption of their previous life have described to me how they did this.

Janet, a university lecturer, managed to return to the same job after a ten-week absence to have her operation. On completing her first week back at work she said:

I find it incredible to think that just ten weeks or so ago I sat in my office anxiously awaiting the outcome of a staff meeting in which my head of department was informing members of staff of my intention.

I can remember the stress and tension as I sat at my desk taking tentative sips at my coffee which I knew I didn't want, but it was something to do. After 45 very slow minutes I could hear the meeting breaking up – now it was make or break time. It seemed an absolute age before the first of them came and told me everything would be all right and that everyone was a hundred per cent behind me. That was the trigger my tear ducts needed and the tears flowed and flowed as the rest of them came one after the other to wish me luck and support.

Throughout the day, everybody I spoke to gave me their full support, each telling me how shocked they were at first, but afterwards saying how the shock turned into respect and even admiration for what I was doing.

I realize I've been extremely lucky and that the gods have been on my side, for a change. But also I do believe I've made an awful lot of luck for myself. I believe my determination and faith in myself have carried me through a very stressful period of my life and have given me the strength to be completely open about myself to everyone at work from top management down to the cleaning ladies.

Another male-to-female transsexual says: 'My son, who is now 20, has been a source of inspiration to me. What strength of character he must have, to cope not only with his mother's death but also to accept the fact that his father is a woman as well.'

Heather, a computer consultant from Scotland, tells how she coped with continuing in the same job, meeting the same clients and living in the same area as when she was a man.

The only time I chickened out was on the first visit to the bank. It was crowded, so I went back to the office and rang the manager. All I had to do was say I was TS. He asked me when I was coming in and I said, 'In about half an hour.' He then said I was to go to the teller on the right and he would have a word with her. Do they train bank managers in this sort of thing? Or do I have an enlightened manager? All other times it has been like falling off a log. For the first time in my life I have felt it was me, not an actor.

One might expect the first couple of weeks to be very stressful. One of the most peculiar things is that even after just a couple of weeks, I cannot imagine what it was like to wear a collar, tie and business suit. It's almost as if 30 years have evaporated.

And Karl, a female-to-male transsexual who has lived all his life in the same house, not merely the same area, says:

I had to explain myself to my fourth consultant boss [Karl works as a hospital administrator] in the same job I have had for 14 years. I had planned to get our working relationship going properly, and I hoped happily, for a month or so before talking about the 'real me', but this was expedited by reason of his inviting me to meet the family. I couldn't face being introduced to the boss's wife as his secretary, as she would naturally expect to see somebody feminine in appearance. So after only three or four days of our knowing each other I had to explain about myself and say that I had no female clothes. He said that his wife would understand perfectly. I am now in my third year of appearing in the right [i.e. masculine] clothes, and although only a few of the staff actually know, I rarely get more than a second look from members of staff. My rapport with all disciplines of staff is certainly enhanced without a doubt.

A few people have found the change-over far easier than they had imagined, or expected, as far as other people's reactions were concerned. Most transsexuals feel that individual attitudes can make or mar any situation. Those who view the whole thing as a self-righting exercise, as Karl did, find they can cope very well. It is, for them, like 'coming out' is for gay people. On the whole, they find that the reaction of workmates is either neutral or favourable, provided a good work reputation has already been built up. Those who manage to continue in the same job usually have a good work record behind them, have put in good service and proved themselves in the original biological sex. All firms are anxious to retain an excellent employee. It is those transsexuals who have a history behind them of instability or disruption who discover that they are not particularly welcome in their new identity.

The hardest task of all is to keep good relationships going with members of the family, who are far more closely involved and attached than colleagues at work. A large majority discover that, sadly, any real links with their families are now over. Possibly a great deal hinges on the quality of the relationship before the change-over. Nowadays, potential transsexuals are advised in the strongest possible terms not to marry, as this will only create problems and will never solve anything. The majority of marriages in which one partner has been a pre-operative transsexual rarely seem to have been happy or close, mainly because the latter is unhappy, confused and depressed prior to changing over. Mostly, also, the marriage was contracted in the first place for the wrong reasons, to enable the future transsexual to feel more ordinary and take a conventional place in society. It is rare that a true affinity had existed to start with, so it is hardly surprising that most relationships cannot survive the change-over.

One male-to-female transsexual explains how her marriage came about:

I knew no eligible women and therefore placed an advert in the personal column of the local paper. I received a reply in due course from a young lady who was obviously as lonely as I.

We went out together for about eighteen months. We seemed to get on with each other and our respective parents and became engaged. I kept telling myself that this is what I am supposed to want. I loved her, of that I have no doubt. I still do, though it was not a physical love and never has been.

The very great bonus for the majority of transsexuals is that somebody comes to love and accept them in their new rôle and becomes a lifetime partner. For some this remains an unattainable dream, but many are now finding that it is not impossible. Though conventional marriages and families may be out, at least for the post-operative transsexual, many manage to establish close, significant and lasting relationships for themselves. The days of isolation and exclusion, of ghetto living, do seem at last to be coming to an end.

CHAPTER 6

Male-to-female transsexuals

When one thinks of transsexuals, a few names such as April Ashley, Christine Jorgensen and Jan Morris immediately spring to mind. These are people who have lived colourful, exotic, exciting and very public lives. They are the 'special' transsexuals, the celebrities. They have also all written books about themselves and their unusual destiny.

But there exist hundreds, possibly thousands, of male-to-female transsexuals whose lives have aroused little, if any, public comment, yet whose experiences are just as strange, just as bizarre, as those of the ones who have become famous. Mostly, the transsexuals who do not become famous are people who prefer to live quietly and without public recognition. But for all of them there is a very real danger that one day their secret will emerge, however much they may try to cover their tracks. This poses questions as to whether transsexuals *should* try to pretend they are normal biological women, or whether they should 'come out' as constructed females, so that nobody, least of all themselves, is under any illusion. Some of the male-to-female transsexuals who have agreed to speak to me for this book are willing to be identified, but others prefer their identity to be kept confidential. Some have managed to pass so successfully as women that nobody in their home town or workplace has any idea that they were once men. And this is the way they want it.

As we saw earlier, transsexualism is not exactly a new phenomenon. Yet it is only over the past forty years or so that men who felt they were really women have been able to make a convincing transformation. As we have also seen, many theories abound as to why transsexualism should have arisen in the first place. Theories vary from the Freudian, which cite over-attachment to and over-identification with the mother as a possible source of the gender dysphoria, to those which suggest that pre-natal hormonal imbalances are the starting-point. The fact is that at present nobody knows for sure what causes the condition. All we do know is that it *does* occur and that it cannot be cured by psychiatric means.

So what are they like, transsexuals? Are they just like you and me, or are they a race apart, a set of people whose background, experiences and ideas bear no relationship to that of the majority? Speaking to a number of these people makes one thing very clear: they have nothing whatever in common with each other apart from their unusual conviction. They are not like Down's Syndrome children, for example, who are immediately recognizable both physically and socially. Transsexuals look and act pretty much like anybody else. If you were to meet one at a party, you would not immediately 'know'. Some transsexuals are nice people, others may be nasty (although I must say I have never met a nasty one). Some are clever, even gifted, while others are of average intelligence and attainments. Some are politically inclined, most are not. Some are gregarious and others are loners. What I am trying to say is that transsexuals are as different from each other as any random selection of people you might see at Waterloo Station in the rush hour. Just as these travellers are all individuals in their backgrounds, political viewpoints and lifestyle, so transsexuals differ widely in their attitude to their condition. They do not represent a united front, as it were, nor are they all agreed on the best form of treatment or medical care.

One of the more colourful of the present-day transsexuals is Rachael Webb. Rachael, who lives in trendy Brixton, is a community worker and a Labour councillor for Ferndale Ward. She was elected in 1986. She has attracted a certain amount of fame – or perhaps notoriety – for her left-wing views, and for her work with lesbian and gay groups. Newspaper reports also accused her of having her sex-change operation, in 1983, 'on the rates'. Since her conversion, Rachael has become a radical feminist and a campaigner for transsexual rights. Her feeling is that transsexuals should not try to pretend they are biological women (or men) but should make it clear to all that they are 'constructed' males or females, in Janice Raymond's phase. This, she feels, will help to destroy the twilight world in which many transsexuals find themselves, to eliminate their ever-present fear of discovery, and to establish transsexuals as people who have a unique contribution to make to the world.

Rachael, now in her mid-forties, was born a biologically normal male; she changed over at the age of 41. She has been married twice and, as a man, fathered four children. For fifteen years she worked as a long-distance lorry-driver, but found it impossible to continue this work as a female. She says she has been confused about her true gender identity for as long as she could remember, and changed over relatively late in life because of her own continuing resistance to accepting herself as a transsexual. She explains:

I've never had a chromosome test, but I must suppose I am a genetically normal male. As a teenager, though, I had a high voice and was very slim and androgynous-looking. I knew from the age of six that I wanted to be a woman when I grew up. Whenever I think back, I can see a very clear picture of myself as a child being absolutely certain that I was a woman.

My parents did want a girl but apart from that they were very traditional people, and I was certainly not treated as a girl. Nor was I brought up in any way as a female.

Rachael says she had little formal education, but educated herself by reading Marx, Engels and the sort of Left Bank existential philosophical works which were popular in the 1950s. She also became a beatnik and a passionate member of CND.

She continues:

At first I thought I must be gay. I knew there was something different about me and that I wasn't quite like other boys. I was very confused and couldn't face up to the fact that I might be transsexual. In those days I took to drugs, in a vain attempt to find myself, to get to the bottom of who I was and come to terms with myself. What I was trying to do, I realize now, was to suppress the transsexuality inside myself. I had the very strong realization that I was living in a world which was completely irrelevant and meaningless to me. The trouble was, I didn't know *how* to make it mean something.

I did start going to a psychiatrist to try and discover just what was wrong. As long ago as 1967 I started having hormone treatment at the Maudsley Hospital in London. Then I began living with a woman and later, when I married, I terminated the treatment. I expect I thought that marriage would make me more 'normal'. I felt I could put all the transsexuality and gender confusion behind me, and live a conventional male life. But eventually I had to say to my wife, 'I can't carry on living like this.' She tried to understand, but found it difficult.

In 1972 I saw another doctor and began hormone treatment again. I later rejected this as well, and tried to carry on as a man. I was working as a long-distance lorry-driver and loved this, as it meant I could be on my own, with my own thoughts. After my first marriage broke up I remarried and had two more children. My new wife knew about the hormone treatment I'd been having.

When my second wife left me in 1978 I then knew I had to face up to myself as a transsexual. For a year I looked after one of my daughters and enjoyed this, though my social worker thought that, as a pre-operative transsexual, I was unfit to be a single parent. It was during this time that I felt I could no longer go on living as a man and that eventually I would have to have the operation. During a night ride to London in winter when there was a three-quarter moon I can remember thinking to myself: I should like to go on doing this work, but to be a woman doing it. Although long-distance lorry-driving doesn't sound a very elevated or intellectual profession, it's one job where you can be absolutely yourself. The paradox is that I couldn't be a woman and do it, because women aren't allowed to be long-distance lorry-drivers.

After having this blinding flash in the middle of the night I went through a paranoid phase. I took this as a need to withdraw into myself. I had been reading a lot of R.D. Laing at the time and he explained that paranoid phases can be a way of dealing with something that cannot easily be handled. At this time I was continuing to look after my 7-year-old daughter.

I found the process of trying to identify myself as a woman very difficult indeed. This is the opinion of every man who wants to be a woman. I then went to see Dr Randell at the Charing Cross, and started treatment in earnest. Dr Randell's definition of a transsexual was somebody who had a lifelong and incurable delusion that they were born into the other sex.

Of course I knew that I was full of contradictions, but as my own life became ever more untenable, I knew I had to do something about myself.

After consulting Dr Randell, Rachael began taking female hormones in earnest and also started electrolysis treatment:

I went through another androgynous phase. I felt then that I wished I didn't have to identify myself either as a man or a woman, but that I could just be a human being where gender didn't matter. In our society, though, that is just not possible. It was this realization which made me a feminist once I had decided to make the change-over.

I had a very strong understanding that women were very deeply oppressed by men. This was something I had certainly not been aware of as a man.

Judy Cousins speaks of a similar realization, in the context of golf clubs. As a male, she had enjoyed golf and belonged to a golf club. 'As far as I was concerned, women were simply an irritation on the golf course,' she said. 'All you wanted was for them to get out of the way when the important matches – the men's – were taking place.' Once she had changed sex she joined the ladies' section of the golf club, and became aware for the first time how strongly women were discriminated against: 'I thought that perhaps I ought to campaign, as it was so unfair, but didn't think I was the right person, somehow.'

Rachael Webb feels that she *is* the right person. Her experiences as both a male and a female, coupled with her political ideology, have convinced her that her only standpoint of integrity is that of a radical feminist. She continues:

I soon realized I was in an extreme minority here. When I first changed over I was living in a small, quiet town in Norfolk, and was the only radical feminist in a total population of 37,000. So I had to move to London, where I became involved in feminism, lesbian and gay groups and local politics.

I've become aware of so many things since the change-over. For one thing, there is a strong element of biological determinism in behaviour. I've now got physical female attributes which mean I move in a different way and that others relate to me differently. With female-type hips you have to walk in a different way and turn your arms outwards. This makes it harder to grip things with your fist. A woman's body-shape means she is far less suited than a man to aggressive behaviour, I've realized. If you say to a woman, 'Make a fist,' she'll usually fold her fingers over nervously. But if you ask a man to do the same thing, he will immediately become aggressive. Men are generally better at bowling and throwing things than women, simply because of their different body-shape.

I have started to realize this since my own body became more female. Hormone treatment has also resulted in my developing female-type breasts, and this makes you hold things in another way. I've noticed from working in offices that a woman will pick up a bundle of files and hold them as if she's nursing a baby. A man, though, would never cradle anything. It's more natural to cradle things when you have breasts.

All these physical things make a major difference to how you regard yourself and also to how others regard you. The physical attributes deeply affect the way we read people. Now that I've become a feminist some radicals have asked me why I felt I needed to make these physical changes to myself, and some feminist groups haven't wanted to accept me as they have taken the attitude that I'm a man trying to infiltrate a woman's world. Janice Raymond makes a similar point in her *Transsexual Empire*.

But I have now come to believe that transsexualism is a physical thing. In the end, I had to change over in order to preserve my sanity, and I have gone to extraordinary lengths, as have all transsexuals, to make that change. I don't ask to be accepted by feminists as a woman, but as a male-to-constructed-female transsexual. I want to make my position completely clear. As a man, I came to feel that all the physical manifestations of my sex were repulsive, but in becoming a woman I have had to relinquish the privileges of the male world. Of course, I do regret this.

When Rachael Webb first decided to make the change-over, she knew she could no longer continue as a long-distance lorry-driver, and so took a TOPS audio-typing course. She recalls:

I was the only 'man' there. I last lived as a man in October 1981 but I had to spend the statutory two years before I could be offered surgery. I never had any problems during that time, though. I used ladies' loos and nobody stared at me or thought me peculiar in any way. My worst problem was my voice. I sounded exactly like a man on the telephone and had to have lots of speech therapy to overcome this – on the NHS, I might add. To me, it was an instantly liberating experience to be able to wear skirts, although I've never been interested in drag, in any way.

But I am aware of the grave disadvantages there are in being a woman. Once I was walking home at eleven o'clock at night and I was picked up. This struck home, and suddenly I realized that from now on it would be difficult to walk home alone at night – something I'd never even thought about before. Also, I haven't felt so free about going into a pub. Apart from the problems associated with being a woman on my own, there is no doubt that the beer doesn't taste the same. It seems as though the oestrogen therapy has had a similar effect to hormones circulating during pregnancy, in that it has made me reject alcohol.

Rachael says that she understands that her desire to be a woman is irrational and knows that she would really be better off as a man. The very worst physical aspect of the change-over, in her opinion, was the electrolysis, which was a 'real nightmare', far worse than the operation itself:

For ages I had to wear heavy make-up to hide the electrolysis scars, which looked like shaving marks. I used to hate myself when I didn't wear make-up as I felt I looked so masculine.

For me, becoming a woman has been like entering a country where I don't know the language. As I was 41 before I began proper treatment, I'd had many years in the male world, and had picked up many male habits and assumptions without really being aware of it. At first I felt it was important to try to be tender and loving and more 'maternal', but now I have the confidence to be myself.

Rachael now feels, contrary to the advice proffered by SHAFT and others, that transsexuals should never play down what they are, any more than a black or gay person should pretend to be, respectively, white or straight. She would like all transsexuals to come out and proclaim themselves for what they are – that is, normal, sane people who have decided on a different destiny for themselves from that which nature gave them. Only then, she feels, will society be able to accept the uniqueness of the transsexual experience and make it meaningful to both men and women. 'If we keep trying to pretend we are "real" men and women, we are furthering the present iniquitous sex stereotyping of our society,' she claims.

And she adds:

The transsexual pulling on her gloves to go to church and wishing she could marry some man so that she can service him is doing more than naïvely adopting a reactionary political stance. She is reinforcing stereotyped gender rôles. She is suffering from the sort of confusion that all of us have to break through if we are to experience our transsexuality as it is and not as society sees men and women.

We have to agree with Janice Raymond when she writes that we are *not* women. This does not mean, however, that we have to accept labels as 'men', but we do have to be clear about what or who we are. When self-knowledge finally does dawn about who we are, when we finally go through the pain, and probably humiliation, of medical treatment, it is in order to again hide and deny who we are.

Rachael says that most transsexuals, after their change-over, 'accept completely and unreservedly all the sexist and heterosexist crap that society uses in order to perpetuate itself. When we do this we pay the price that women have paid for generations and generations.'

She has made an eloquent plea to other transsexuals not to fool people that they are women when they are not. This, she says, stops us from effectively denying that we are men. 'We transsexuals,' says Rachael, 'have nothing to gain from our attempts to gain legitimacy and respectability from the medical profession. We confuse ourselves and other people by trying to adopt a false identity, and pretending that we are real women (or men, in the case of female-to-male transsexuals).'

Rachael Webb is very 'modern', indeed avant-garde, in her approach, and many transsexuals would not go along with her views. She has adopted what many view as an extreme standpoint, because she feels this is the only ideologically tenable position. Most others, however, prefer to hide the fact of their sex-change from their colleagues and workmates, confiding only in those few friends and relatives who absolutely have to know.

But, as observed earlier, there is always the possibility

that the transsexual will be found out. However much a person tries to hide the fact that he or she has changed sex, the minute there is any publicity of any kind it can virtually be guaranteed that somebody will spill the beans and the secret will be common knowledge.

This is what happened to Adèle Anderson, of the all-girl singing group Fascinating Aida. She managed to keep her secret for many years, mainly by keeping a low profile working in the civil service. As she began her change-over at the age of 20, before she had fully entered the male world as an adult, and before she had become very masculine in appearance, she made an extremely convincing transition. But although she had worked as a civil servant since leaving university, she had always nurtured an ambition to be a singer and when she heard there were auditions for a new, raunchy, all-girl singing group, she decided to go along.

The original impact she made is described by Dillie Keane, founder of the group. In her book, *Fascinating Who?*, Dillie writes:

Then she sang for us and I'll never forget it. She placed the music in front of me and I started to play the song which was, I recall, in E♭. I nearly fell off my stool when she sang the whole thing an octave lower.

'What's your range?' I asked in amazement when she'd got through the song.

Adèle, Dillie recalls, replied by vocalizing her entire range – nearly five octaves. Dillie decided that anybody that eccentric should be given a fair hearing, and so started talking to her about herself. A small niggling doubt that formed in the back of Dillie's mind grew and eventually could not be contained any longer.

There was something odd about her, something slightly bizarre. She seemed to be an anachronism, and reminded me of the pre-war cabarets in Berlin. Her height and her basso-profundo voice puzzled us.

At last Nica voiced the awful question. 'Adèle, I have to ask you something,' she said awkwardly. 'Are you a man?' It wasn't a subtle question, but how the hell can you be subtle about something like that?

Adèle went pink and looked mortified and wounded, as though we'd asked her if she was a thief or a sneak. 'No,' she said after a moment . . . of course, as we found out later, Adèle was a transsexual . . . I don't know if we would have chosen her if we'd known. Transsexuals don't get a great press, and I'm not sure we'd have been that brave. I'm glad now we didn't know, because we were never faced with that dilemma, and chose her simply because she was right. As she herself said, she was the best man for the job.

In the same book, Adèle herself writes:

When Dillie rang me to say I'd got the job my heart leapt and almost immediately sank like a stone. This was an all-girl group. Did the fact that I was transsexual automatically disqualify me? I consulted several friends, all of whom said, 'Certainly not. For many years you've lived as a woman and worked as a woman. Why view this job differently from any other?'

Adèle goes on to say that sometimes being a transsexual can feel like being an ex-prisoner. You finished your sentence years ago, yet you are never allowed to forget that once you spent time inside. She continues:

There are members of the public who feel that's right, that you should *never* be allowed to forget, but I don't subscribe to that viewpoint. I paid my debt to society with the twenty years I was forced to spend it as a male, and I don't wish to be constantly reminded of it. Since I shall spend the rest of my life living as a female I do not see why I should have to set myself apart from other women and think of myself as 'second-class'.

Adèle, then, is very different from Rachael Webb, who does not see herself as a second-class female, but as a constructed – i.e. not a biological – woman.

Adèle changed over in 1973 and, like so many transsexuals in Britain beat a path to John Randell's door at the Charing Cross Hospital. She takes up the story:

I used to turn up at Randell's clinic for psychiatric assessment. At first he told me I was too aggressive and that I'd have to quieten down if I was serious about becoming a female. Then he told me I was too masculine as I would turn up wearing jeans. When I once turned up wearing a dress I was told I was overdoing the feminine bit. I know that he had very fixed and traditional ideas about what was male and what was female, and he always wanted transsexuals to go in for very traditional occupations.

All my life I had felt as if I was a terribly weak male, partly because I never wanted to be a boy. The thing I hate is when people tell me I spent the first twenty years of my life as a man, as I never felt I reached manhood. I thought of myself as being a very feminine boy, but my voice did give me away. I had to have a lot of speech therapy and work very hard on my voice so that I didn't sound masculine. I soon realized that there is nothing simple about changing over. When I first started to have treatment, I overdid being feminine, and one of my friends told me I sat down just like the Queen. I tried to do everything properly, and it just didn't look natural.

Now, I'm more or less as I was at eighteen, but with the right sort of body. I can be myself and not bother about whether I am acting feminine or masculine. I must say that the younger you do it, the easier it is from a physical point of view, and the more convincing you can look. Also, I hadn't fully entered the man's world and I hadn't picked up lots of masculine habits and gestures that it would be hard to shed.

Now, I don't look butch but I do look boyish. Although I was a feminine-looking boy, I have become a boyish-looking woman.

Adèle, however, has no interest in being self-consciously feminine or passive, and has retained an aggression, or assertiveness, which she feels stands her in good stead. 'I didn't stand any nonsense from Randell,' she said.

In my job I was used to responsibility and having to deal with people, so, without being rude, I gave as good as I got.

I'm not the most aggressive one in Aida – that's the job of our leader. She's the one who screams and shouts, and that came as a relief to me. She's always prepared to stand up and fight for the good of the group. But in my personal relationships I've found I prefer it if I can be the stronger partner. I never had a relationship as a male, but now I feel I can have proper partnerships. Mostly, my lovers are younger than me and I feel I help them to grow up. I would, though, find it very difficult to go out with a dominant man. And I am absolutely convinced that I do not want to get married and have children – I've never wanted that.

Adèle says that, for her, life has become a hundred per cent better since changing over.

I took stock of my situation at the age of 21, and felt I had to do it there and then. I was certain that I would not be able to achieve as a male and I didn't want to adopt the solution of many transsexuals, which is to throw themselves wholeheartedly into an ultra-masculine world. I felt that if I didn't make the change-over while I was still young, and before I had embarked on a career or partnership, I would gradually become more and more unhappy with myself. It seems odd to me now that so many male-to-female transsexuals get married and have children – that I've never been able to understand – and also that they try to be ridiculously masculine.

The surgery, she says wryly, is no joke and not to be recommended for people who are not absolutely serious about the whole thing:

I wouldn't have been one of the pioneers. I'm sure I would never have been able to go in for the surgery unless I knew in advance that it would be entirely successful. I wouldn't have wanted to come out neither one thing nor the other. I do feel strongly about the laws relating to transsexuals, and I hate the way we are lumped together with gays. For instance, the main reason we can't get married as transsexuals is that a lot of people say that if we are allowed to get married, then gays will be able to get married to each other, so that in the end the institution of marriage will become a complete mockery.

Everybody knows I am a transsexual now, because of the publicity surrounding our singing group. Otherwise, I don't expect I would have gone around telling everybody. But I know there are transsexuals who don't tell anybody, not even their partners. I think this is unfair on the partner. Marriage doesn't concern me personally as I have never wanted to get married, though I was brought up in a very conventional household. But I still think the laws are discriminatory and prejudicial. People remain prejudiced against transsexuals, although this is fading to some extent.

Dora, a Canadian transsexual, does not want to be identified. She says that hardly any of her clients, in her job as a computer consultant, know that she was once a man, and she would prefer it to stay that way. Dora undertook the whole business of her sex-change very methodically. She decided to change over in 1981, and felt that the best solution was a complete change of lifestyle and location. She explains:

Before I changed over I had already established a working relationship with a man and he was very supportive. I came to a decision to stop fighting my true identity and establish myself as completely as possible in the female gender. So I left my job and decided to go to university as a mature student.

I had a letter from the gender-identity clinic I was attending to say what my situation was. I had changed over in the two months before going to university and was still having to come to terms with this dramatic change in my life. As far as one can, I had thought the whole thing through. When I was accepted at university, I sold my house and moved to another place. I thought that it was best to reincarnate myself as completely as possible, as it were. Obviously a few people knew about it, but not many.

Dora says that, as a transsexual, she tends towards feminism:

When you grow up as a male, you are not indoctrinated into dependency, and there you have a great advantage. But people do expect me to be more incompetent now that they perceive me as a woman. Also, you do feel freer to admit when you can't cope. As a man, you would try to bluster your way through and be reluctant to admit incompetence in any area. I like to keep a low profile and don't want to be noticed. I find that if you give people visual fulfilment of what to expect, they don't look further.

I don't go out of my way to look odd, though as I am over six feet tall I have to be very careful. Mostly I wear very ordinary clothes that don't draw attention, and as I do a lot of sailing I wear tracksuits quite often. Occasionally, people do look at me in rather an odd way. I wonder, is it because I'm wearing a nice dress, because I'm tall for a woman, or because I've been rather aggressive? I'm also wondering: are they reading me, have they become suspicious?

Dora calls herself a feminist, and says that when at university she went on many feminist, consciousness-raising courses:

In the early days I thought that to be feminine and feminist was a contradiction. Now, I realize you can be both, but I don't perceive feminism as being necessarily allied to the radical left. I would call myself a caring capitalist. I have my own business, am not financially dependent on anybody, and am ambitious for myself. In that sense I'm a feminist. I do, though, have a very

113

close and permanent husband-and-wife type relationship with a man.

I am always aware of the duality in my nature, and feel that I should be able to take advantage of it. I've had a very special experience and ought really to be able to combine the best of both worlds – the independence of men with the sensitivity of women. I am sure this helps me in my work and when dealing with clients. But my years as a man have also given me confidence in myself, a feeling that I can achieve, support myself and be independent if I want to be.

I felt that to play the male rôle was a strain. Over the past few years [Dora is now approaching 40] I have felt able to relax and be myself. For the first time in my life, I feel comfortable. I also feel that if I have to make a decision, I can say that I'm not quite sure. As a man, I would have felt extremely peculiar about saying that. I felt, and most transsexuals feel, that as men they are playing a rôle to which they are not really suited, even though most of us manage it fairly competently.

I think the most graphic way I can describe how I felt wrong as a man was that every morning, when I woke up and looked at myself in the mirror, I saw a stranger. I got a shock that the kind of body which reflected itself back at me was not conforming to my inner concept of myself. Now if I look in the mirror I know what to expect and I no longer get a shock. My body-shape is in accord with my mental picture of myself.

Dora's job involves going to large companies and advising them on their computer needs.

'I definitely think my height helps me in my work,' she said. 'It gives me an air of authority. Because I changed my location, job and lifestyle, I've had no problems at all in re-entering society.'

Usually, transsexuals who are married have to get divorced before they embark on any irreversible treatment. Indeed, most gender-identity clinics will not recommend a particular patient for treatment unless he or she is first single in law. This often means that the transsexual effectively loses sight of his or her family, and may never have proper contact with them again. This has not happened in Alison's case, however. At the time of writing Alison, aged 38, is still a pre-operative transsexual, living full-time as a woman and waiting for an operation on the NHS. All her documents have been changed to the new name but she has not divorced and is in fact still living with her legal wife Janice.

Owing to some strange twist in the law, Alison is not going to get divorced, either, and intends to carry on living with her original partner in a sisterly relationship similar to that of Rae and Isabel Smith, described earlier. How has she managed it?

'It's not really due to me, but to Janice,' Alison, a former publican now running a self-help organization, told me. 'What my wife has had to put up with is amazing. I am so lucky.'

Alison married very young – at eighteen – and now has two grown-up sons. She decided to change over when they were aged sixteen and fourteen:

When they were young, I tried my best to be a proper father. It got harder and harder over the years until at last I couldn't hide it any longer. When the boys were small, I managed to conceal the fact that I wanted to be a woman. I made a determined effort.

Janice knew quite soon after we were married that I liked to dress up in woman's clothes, but even so it was a shock to her when she realized that one day I would want to live properly and full-time as a woman. I managed to keep it from her for a time, but in the end, of course, she had to know. It's nothing short of a miracle that she has stayed with me.

Most transsexuals' relationships break up, reckons Alison, because the woman starts to lose everything she had married a man for – sex, a protector, a breadwinner, a companion of the opposite gender:

Society still judges men as providers and breadwinners. That is still the main reason women marry us. All that is thrown out of the window when a husband suddenly announces that from now on he wants to live as a woman and actually become a woman. It is the most earth-shattering news a woman can receive, and very few want to have anything to do with the man after that. The woman usually wants the transsexual husband to disappear out of her life permanently. But my relationship survived. Partly, I think, it was because Janice knew about me and had accepted me for many years.

Of course our relationship has changed completely. We were husband and wife but now we are close friends.

Alison has decided to call herself 'Mrs' – which means that in her house there are two 'married women' living together. 'When we get dental appointments, for example,' Alison says, 'they are addressed to Mrs A. and Mrs J. Legally, we are man and wife and always will be. Whatever effect the hormones have, and whatever cosmetic changes are made to my body, the legal sex won't alter.'

Alison and Janice's continuing closeness is underlined by the fact that they still share the same bed. 'I have been having hormone treatment for two years, and so cannot perform sexually as a man, even though I am still pre-operative,' explains Alison. 'I am also having regular electrolysis – the only person in Britain, I believe, to be having it under the NHS. In many ways, my situation is unique, and I've been extremely lucky. Even when I've had the operation, I shan't get divorced.'

Alison says that the boys, now aged twenty and eighteen, have taken it all very well, especially as it happened in a very public way.

When I first began living full-time as a woman, I was running a pub in a very small village in Cornwall, and so everybody knew. There was no possible way of hiding it from the people in the village. My younger son came to terms with it particularly well, and since the change-over has never called me anything but Alison. He say he's had no problems with his friends, and neither of the boys has ever complained.

I realize that my situation is anomalous, both legally and socially, and always will be. For instance, if I was walking along a lane at night with two other women and we were all raped, the other two would be able to sue, but I wouldn't. I would just have to accept it, as in this aspect of the law I shall continue to be male. But even though there are many peculiarities remaining, I feel far happier now than I did when I tried to live as a man. As I have always worn women's clothes, it's not a new thing for Janice and me to go shopping together. The most wonderful thing is that we have been able to keep the family together, and that we are all able to get on well.

In my case, it is entirely due to the understanding of my wife. She has had to cope with me changing my appearance and body-shape totally. Whereas she looks the same to me as she always has done, to her I look completely different, like another person.

One of the worst problems male-to-female transsexuals have to face is that if they have lost their hair there are no tried and tested treatments to bring it back, any more than there are for ordinary biological males. Many transsexuals wear wigs, but of course this solution is less satisfactory than having your own hair. Alison was one of the very first people in Britain to try a new hair treatment called Regaine, a scalp lotion which appears to be the first hair-restorer that actually works. The active ingredient is in fact a drug used to lower blood pressure. It was found that the substance, Minodixil, caused hair to grow back on the heads of some men who took it for blood-pressure problems.

This led the manufacturers to wonder if it could be used as a hair-restorer when applied directly to the head. Trials began, and many men did indeed grow hair again, after being bald. The treatment is very expensive and is not effective for everybody, but it worked wonders for Alison. She said:

I started using it in 1984, after I had developed a bald patch and had a very receding hairline. My hair started to recede in my mid-twenties and followed the classic male baldness pattern. After nearly three years the bald patch has gone and I no longer have a receding hairline. To me, it's been a wonderful blessing as I now have a proper female head of hair and I can go to the hairdressers.

If the treatment really does live up to its promise, it could become standard for those male-to-female transsexuals who have started to lose their hair.

Melanie Jane Martin had her operation in June, 1987, and is less lucky than Alison in that her marriage has not been able to survive her transsexuality. An artist, Melanie Jane is aged 32, living full-time as a woman, and has stayed in the same flat she lived in before the change-over.

Melanie Jane told me:

I got married basically because I didn't realize things were as wrong with me as I later discovered. I knew from childhood that there was something amiss but imagined it would right itself as I got older. I can remember thinking as I stood at the altar during my wedding that at last I had made it as a man. I stood there congratulating myself because I had managed to acquire a wife. We had a lovely wedding, a really big do, but it wasn't long before everything started going wrong with the relationship.

As soon as my marriage broke up it became clear to me that I was a transsexual and that I had to make the change-over. Actually, if I had been honest with myself, I would have admitted that I had known since the age of eight, when I said to my mother that I would like to be a mummy one day. I can remember my mother's answer. She said, 'Don't be so ridiculous.' I sensed that she was almost disgusted by what I said. I felt disgusted with myself as soon as I had said it because I knew it could never happen.

But though Melanie Jane wanted to be a woman, as a man she was extremely masculine; she became a heavy-metal enthusiast and a biker, weighting seventeen stone and with a big straggly beard:

To tell you the truth, I looked exactly like Giant Haystacks. I had long hair and was always underneath cars. I've always loved cars. Since my change-over, people tell me I look like Paula Yates – a complete transformation. I lost four stone in four months and went through a period of the most enormous upheaval.

I have been living full-time as a woman since 5 February 1985. By the time I changed over my divorce had gone through, so there was nothing to stop me any more. My neighbours have been watching me change from this ugly ape of a man into a petite and quite attractive woman. Now, it doesn't occur to me that I ever was a man, and the only outward reminder I have is that I still need a lot of electrolysis. Oh, the dreadful electrolysis! It is without doubt the worst aspect of the whole transformation.

I came back from one electrolysis session and went to the pub in the evening with all these lumps and bumps all over my face. I expected everybody to stare at me in horror, but nobody took any notice, which just shows how much is in the mind. Instantly I started to live full-time as a woman I felt right, whereas I had always felt wrong before. It must be wonderful to be a man if you can be, but my mind won't tell me that I am.

Unlike many transsexuals, Melanie Jane does not want to hide her background or be anonymous:

I've stayed in the same place and kept all the same friends. I have also kept the same interests. I have always loved vintage and classic cars, and have collected them. I had my present car, a metallic blue Ford Granada, when I looked very different, and nobody has ever taken any notice. I have made the most dramatic transformation anybody can make, and nobody has taken a blind bit of notice. It's quite amazing, really, and makes me wonder how many of the so-called problems some transsexuals have about re-entering society are actually all in their minds.

Becoming a woman has, Melanie Jane said, given her far more confidence than ever before:

Just last year in Majorca I went bathing topless. I wouldn't even go on the beach before. My main physical problem is walking, as if I'm not careful I tend to mince along, and that is a dead giveaway as it doesn't look feminine at all. I have had to consciously undo my masculine walk, and it has been quite difficult.

Melanie Jane is convinced that transsexuality begins in the womb:

It is the only explanation that fits. It's a pity transsexuals have been lumped together with homosexuals and transvestites because the popular belief is that gays and TVs [transvestites] would become transsexuals but for a push. But the genuine transsexual knows that he is not a TV, and is always aware of the difference. To be a transsexual is not the same as living permanently in women's clothes, and all transsexuals know this.

The best thing is that all my friends and acquaintances have been so supportive. I am now in the last stages of selling off my collection of vintage cars and am getting good wishes from everyone. Recently, I had a letter from a contact in New York who began by apologizing for not knowing what to call me, and then wished me the best of luck in my new life. Nobody has been nasty. My only regret is that I never had children from my marriage. Although my wife – quite rightly – accused me of having no sex drive, I would have loved children, and always wanted them.

The very best thing for me is that my artistic ability has returned. I attended a very good art school but never put my training to use as I never seemed to have anything to say. Now that I have managed at last to establish my identity, I am recovering that ability I thought I had lost. I have the very strong feeling that I have missed ten years of my life, and have a lot to make up. I think that in a woman's world it is easier to be yourself. Not that I'm saying it's necessarily better to be a woman, and outwardly there is nothing particularly appealing about the female condition. But I'm not playing an artificial part any more. As far as I'm concerned, I am now me for the first time.

A transsexual who has hit the headlines recently is Keith Hull, who has now been surgically transformed into the glamorous Stephanie Ann Lloyd. An interview in *Sunday* magazine showed Stephanie in a teeny yellow bikini – and, overleaf, a picture of her topless. Like most successful transsexuals, Stephanie looks like a completely normal woman. Unlike most, however, Stephanie has married in her new sex and now lives happily with her husband David. The couple had to marry in Sri Lanka, as, of course, the ceremony is not legal in Britain.

As a man, Keith Hull was a successful businessman. Pictures of him taken before his sex change show a confident-looking executive wearing dark glasses and a tailored suit. Keith was also married, and the father of three children. Gradually, in the course of the change-over process, Keith managed to lose everything he had – his job, his home, his wife and family. This, as we know, is a not uncommon experience for male-to-female transsexuals.

Stephanie, who now runs a highly profitable business selling clothes and other items specially made for transsexuals, anticipates a £2 million turnover in 1987. She has Transformation shops in London and Manchester, and also a hotel, Transformation Changeways, where men wishing to dress and act as women can do so in complete privacy and comfort. All clothes are provided. Stephanie also runs a mail-order business, and has recently emerged as a very public transsexual.

In appearance, she is the epitome of the successful businesswoman, with abundant dark hair (a wig, for as Keith Hull she had already started thinning on top) and casual but stylish clothes.

She said:

When I first told my firm that I was transsexual, and having treatment to be able to live as a woman, [my boss] asked for 24 hours to think about it. He was flabbergasted.

Then one day I left with my briefcase and came back a few months later already transformed, and wearing a wig, make-up and skirt. Most of my colleagues were wonderful, but then the whole thing hit the headlines and it became impossible for me to carry on. I was creating such a stir I couldn't go out. I couldn't work, and the chairman said sadly that it would be better if I left. So I went.

Overnight I went from being a successful marketing manager to being out of work.

If Keith had thought his wife would understand and stick by him, he was mistaken: 'I knew I could look after myself, so within a week I went to my solicitor and signed everything I owned over to Marie — the house, the lot. I ended up with just 78p in my pocket — nowhere to live and nowhere to go.'

Like most male-to-female transsexuals, Keith Hull found that sex with his wife became impossible and, again like most, tried everything to sort his marriage out and become 'normal'. But in the end, there were only two alternatives: to live henceforward as a woman, as completely as possible, or to die.

Stephanie says now, that after the years of hell trying to come to terms with the dilemma, it is as if she has stepped from black and white into glorious technicolor. 'I'd always been a woman inside,' she said, 'but I'd been living life like a pantomime person. And when they put me back together again, it seemed like simply the most natural thing in the world.'

By far the great majority of stories in this book are positive, and tell of transsexuals who have been, despite all the pain, expense, physical and mental agony involved in the change-over, far happier in their chosen sex than ever they were in the original biological one. But, it must be said, not all stories end on a happy note: there are sometimes casualties.

I first met Anna Heming about fifteen years ago in a Richmond pub. Originally Albert, and a seaman, Anna had undergone a sex-change operation some years before

121

in Switzerland, after castrating herself. As a man, she also had many tattoos which did not exactly add credibility to her wish to be a woman. However, she effected a successful change-over and set up an electrical and second-hand goods shop in Bristol. She also made electronic organs (the musical instruments in this case) in her spare time, and devoted much energy to helping other transsexuals, particularly young ones.

I remember Anna as a very witty person, in a rather rough seaman's way. As we were sitting down in the pub, she suddenly said: 'Do you like my bosom?'

'Yes,' I replied, wondering what was coming next.

'It's false,' she announced. 'The real one's in my handbag.'

Anna had with her a young transsexual friend, Pauline, and the two spent much time discussing the inadequacies of Pauline's artificial vagina.

'With the size of my present vagina, I could only have an affair with a budgerigar,' Pauline said.

Anna commented, 'It's no good to man or beast, what she's got.'

As we talked I learned about Anna's life. She, like most transsexuals, had always felt herself to be female but had nevertheless married, had children, and followed a very masculine occupation. She had her sex-change operation in 1959 and eventually divorced in 1971. Since living full-time as a woman, Anna had managed to combine both masculine and feminine occupations – according to our present stereotypes. She both made her own clothes and had built her own house, brick by brick. For her, there was no incongruity in doing the most masculine of jobs.

'In fact, I'm more able to build walls and electronic organs now that I'm a woman,' she told me.

In 1981, however, I read in a Bristol paper that Anna had committed suicide, aged 68. The final irony was that on her death certificate Anna's sex was given as male. At the inquest her son Johann, aged 33, said: 'She couldn't keep up the façade in her own mind. It wasn't her appearance, but she was getting old. She would never have confided this to anyone but the family, and she would have been horrified to know she was registered dead as a male.'

Johann explained that Anna had been suffering from depression since retiring from her shop, and had been receiving treatment at a local hospital. Anna was found dead by her son, with a plastic bag over her head, in a back bedroom. There were two suicide notes.

Transsexuals, like humankind in general, differ widely from each other in experience and attitudes. Most manage to make an effective change, and to establish a workable lifestyle for themselves, but of course it doesn't always happen. There are tragedies and misfits, people who will never finally decide what or who they are, and who will never be able to come to terms with themselves. Gender-identity clinics are supposed to be able to sort out those who would benefit from treatment, and those who simply have an incurable mental disorder, but of course they cannot always be accurate. And, as Rachael Webb says, the psychiatrists who run the clinics have in the main bought the current sex stereotypes and orthodoxy which stipulate that women are like this and men are like that, and that there is a wide gap between the two sexes.

Mostly, the pioneer transsexuals did not bother themselves much about the stereotypes. All they knew was that somehow they had to become women (or men), and if that meant accepting the way society currently viewed the sexes, then that was part of the continuing price they had to pay. It is probably the case that many early transsexuals *did* try to force themselves into rôles for which they were not suited, and attempted to live out other people's ideas of what a 'real' man or woman did. Now that there are so many, and now that the subject has come out into the open, an increasing number of transsexuals feel that they can be themselves and are gaining confidence in their situation.

Rachael Webb's views now sound extreme, partly because they are allied, as Dora has said, to the radical left, and by no means all transsexuals are politically inclined. But at the end of the day she is probably right. Transsexuals are not 'real' men and women, any more than black people are 'really' white. By pretending to be genuine men or women, transsexuals are trying to deny that they have a special, unusual existence, in that they are actually of both sexes. If they admitted it, according to Rachael Webb, they could play a significant part in society by helping to overcome our present stereotypes, which are still putting individuals into straitjackets. It would perhaps be less trouble if those with transsexual inclinations could be persuaded not to change their bodies, but to accept themselves as they were born. For the moment, however, this remains a fantasy, and so far very few have managed this; at present the best treatment seems to be surgery and hormones. None the less transsexuals could surely, if they 'came out' more, do a lot to bridge the gap between the sexes.

CHAPTER 7

Female-to-male transsexuals

It is commonly believed that there are far fewer female-to-male transsexuals than there are the other way round. Gender-identity clinics usually put the ratio at about one to four, going on the proportions of women-to-men that they see.

The truth is that nobody really knows whether the phenomenon manifests itself more often in biological men, or whether it is simply that fewer biological women seek surgery and treatment for their condition. Certainly SHAFT knows of several women living full-time as men who have never had any kind of medical or hormonal treatment at all, and very few outsiders ever suspect these are not 'real' men. Moreover, as fewer female-to-male transsexuals go public, it is almost impossible to ascertain how common a condition it is. It is however widely acknowledged that throughout history many high-achieving women have passed themselves off as men, or have dressed as men in order to gain access to the male world and, by implication, male rank and privileges. But were people like Joan of Arc true female-to-male transsexuals? It is very hard to tell, from the standpoint of the twentieth century, how such people saw themselves. Then there were various women who joined the navy, able to pass as boys in seamen's clothing; and the strange case of Dr James Miranda Barry, whose entire working life was spent as a man. An army surgeon who travelled all over the world, he died in 1865 and was proclaimed to be a perfect female by the woman who laid him out.

Probably the first female-to-male transsexual of modern times – though she never had any transformational surgery – was the novelist Radclyffe Hall, author of the notorious novel *The Well of Loneliness* (published in 1928). Radclyffe, always called 'John' by her friends and close circle, was born in 1886, an only child, and inappropriately christened Marguerite. She realized early in life that she was somehow different and would never become a wife and mother, the standard and almost the only career available to women of her class and time. She was fortunate in that she came from a rich family and was well educated. At the age of 21 she inherited a fortune which meant she never had to work or be dependent on anyone for the rest of her life. From that age to her mid-thirties she travelled a lot and lived, in her own words, a life of complete idleness. Her lover at the time was the society hostess Mabel Batten, usually called Ladye, who was many years older than John.

While Ladye was still alive, John fell in love with Una, Lady Troubridge, who, at the age of 28, gave up her husband, family and conventional life to live with Radclyffe Hall as her permanent lover and companion. Una and John considered themselves spiritually married, and on her tombstone Una had carved these words: 'Una Troubridge, the friend of Radclyffe Hall.'

After meeting Una, John got down to work in earnest and became a prolific and prize-winning novelist. She was also something of a womanizer, and, much to Una's distress, had several affairs during her lifelong friendship with Una. The partnership was able to survive these vicissitudes, however. The couple's union seemed to follow a fairly conventional husband-and-wife pattern, given that they were two women living together. They exchanged rings, and Una became very much the supportive partner, subjugating her own considerable artistic talent to look after John and allow her genius (as Una saw it) to flourish. John was the breadwinner, the man, the more important one, the partner whose wishes and desires always had to come first. Una saw herself as the housewife, looking after the domestic side of their nomadic life together. Radclyffe Hall's most famous novel, *The Well of Loneliness*, is a sympathetic study of lesbianism, and became the subject of one of the most celebrated literary trials of the century. After the court case it was banned for obscenity, but was later published in America. The editor of a popular newspaper, the London *Daily*

Express, said at the time that he would rather give a child prussic acid than this book to read.

The Well of Loneliness cannot be considered great literature, and Virginia Woolf castigated it as Radclyffe Hall's 'worthy dull book'. It does, however, give a detailed description through the life of the heroine, Stephen Gordon, of what it was like to be a sexual 'invert', in the language of the day.

The main obscenity contained in the book seems to be the one line 'and that night they were not divided', which denotes that Stephen Gordon at last sleeps with her lover, Mary Llewellyn. The judges held that the book described an unnatural and perverted passion.

In his biography of Una Troubridge, Richard Ormrod writes:

John, who called herself a 'congenital invert' (in the terminology of her day, emanating from Havelock Ellis), would now be more correctly recognized (in the terminology of today) as a female-to-male 'transsexual' (a term first coined by Dr Harry Benjamin in 1949, six years after her death): that is, as a genetic female (XX chromatin) with a psychosexual male identity, with some secondary physical androgyny ... Her self-image was largely masculine ('I can't feel that I am a woman') and was mirrored in her appearance, behaviour and life-long adoption of the name John. 'Transsexuality' is a post-war phenomenon in terms of research and resources, largely due to the invention of synthetic sex-hormones and advances in plastic and reconstructive surgery. In addition, research into endrocrinology and psychology by such pioneers as C.N. Armstrong of Newcastle now postulate that where there is any disharmony between the four primary criteria of sex-determination (chromosomal, gonadal, hormonal and psychological) there is, in effect, a state of 'intersex' ...

It is tempting to wonder whether John, had she lived now, would have undergone sexual reassignment surgery, to produce secondary male characteristics, to enable her to live as a man. She already had a prepossessing deep voice, only slight feminine contours, and a phallic sexuality, all of which would have made it a very short step to take. If it had been available to her as an option, would she have sought the surgeon's knife to bring body more into harmony with mind and spirit, her nature with her possibilities? Could she indeed have said no to the possibility, in relative terms, of the healing of her, as she saw it, 'maimed and insufferable body'?

Her gender dichotomy (the sense of having a man's mind in a woman's body) and its attendant angst was perhaps neither a big catastrophe nor a small annoyance, but somewhere between the two; and her power of endurance was positively heroic, particularly in the last three years of her life.

Radclyffe Hall died in 1943 of bowel cancer, at the age of 57, having worked like a maniac during the last phase of her life, perhaps to make up for the thirty-odd years she considered herself to have spent in idleness before. All the time she was devotedly nursed by Una, who continued to write to 'my John' every day for the rest of her long life. Although she considered herself sexually abnormal, Radclyffe Hall made no attempt to look or act like an ordinary woman, and her close-cropped hair and mannishly tailored clothes told the world in no uncertain terms how she saw herself. She had all the advantages that class, money and talent could give her, and she was also lucky enough to find a lifelong, devoted lover in Una Troubridge. Other female-to-male transsexuals of this century have not been so fortunate.

The first female-to-male transsexual to have modern surgery and hormone treatment was Michael Dillon, who was christened Laura and brought up by two maiden aunts, Daisy and Toto, on the south coast of England. Dillon's transformation was carried out in 1948 by Sir Harold Gillies, the famous Australian plastic surgeon, and the techniques he formulated for the creation of an artificial penis and scrotum are still in use today.

As a child Laura Dillon was tomboyish and clever. She was born on 1 May 1915 and orphaned at an early age. Her mother died when she was only ten days old, and her father when she was ten. Her father was the seventh baronet of Lismullen, in the south of Ireland. Laura went to Oxford in 1933 and became president of the Ladies' Boat Club. She became increasingly unhappy as a woman and wondered whether anything could be done to transform her into a man. She confided to close friends that, like Radclyffe Hall, she had never felt like a woman, and responded like a male to other people. She first made

Christine Jorgensen, formerly GI George Jorgensen, the world's first surgically transformed male-to-female transsexual, pictured in 1970 in America and, below, in about 1975.

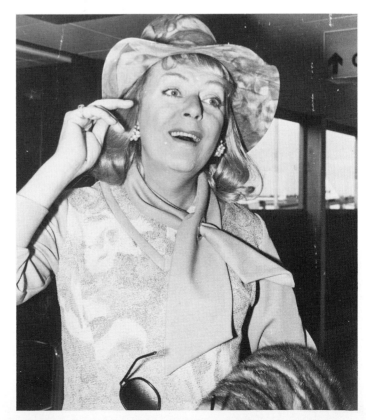

April Ashley, formerly merchant seaman George Jamieson, in 1970, when she worked as a model.

Tennis-player Renée Richards, now Martina Navratilova's mentor, pictured in 1977 playing Virginia Wade in the US Open Competition at Forest Hills, New York. Dr Richards was defeated 6-1, 6-4. Miss Wade won Wimbledon that year.

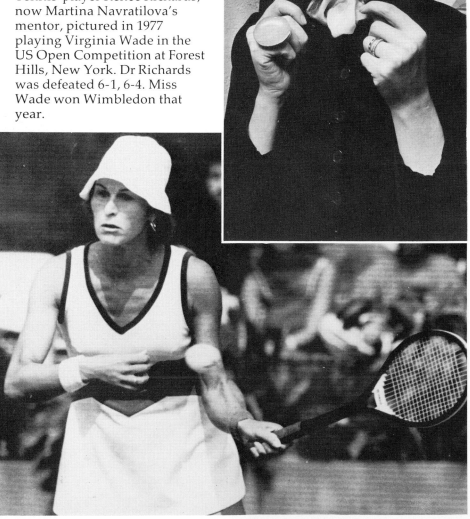

	Bearer Titulaire	Wife Femme
Occupation / Profession	Lorry Driver	
Place of birth / Lieu de naissance	Uphill	
Date of birth / Date de naissance	25·5·40	
Residence / Résidence	Great Britain	
Height / Taille	5 ft. 10½ in.	ft. in.
Distinguishing marks / Signes particuliers		

CHILDREN *ENFANTS*

Name Nom	Date of birth Date de naissance	Sex Sexe

Bearer
Titulaire

Wife
Femme

Photo

The bearer (and wife, if included) should sign opposite on receipt

Part of the
passport of Tim
Webb, lorry
driver,
showing him
immediately
prior to the
change-over, in
1981.

Rachael Webb,
Labour
councillor for
Ferndale Ward,
Brixton, in
1987. *Picture:
Crissie Patient.*

Judy Cousins as Lewen, officer in the Indian Army, 1942.

Lewen in 1966.

Judy Cousins as she is today.

Judy Cousins with one of her grandchildren in 1975.

George Martin in 1981, looking like 'Giant Haystacks'.

Holiday snaps of Melanie Jane Martin taken in 1986.

Below: Laura Dillon in 1938, aged 23 (Foreign Office photograph) and right, on the right, with friend (about 1937).

Laura Dillon as a young girl, early 1930s.

Below left: Laurence Michael Dillon pictured just after his sex-change operation, in about 1948.

Below right: Michael Dillon with Daisy, the aunt who brought him up, in 1950.

Above left: Michael Dillon as a ship's doctor, 1955, and, above right, out of uniform in the same year.

Right: holiday snap of Dillon, 1955.

Below: Dillon as Lobzang Jivaka, Buddhist monk. Taken at Rizong Gompa, Ladakh, shortly before his death.

↓

Top left: Brenda Rees, aged sixteen; top right, in WRNS uniform, aged 22.

Above: Mark Rees working at his typewriter, 1987; (left) portrait of Mark Rees.

enquiries about sex-change treatment in 1939, when aged 23, but got nowhere.

She managed to meet a sympathetic doctor in 1942, but was not able to start making a permanent transformation until 1945, when she met Sir Harold Gillies. He performed many operations on Dillon until at last, in 1948, Laura Maude Dillon formally became Laurence Michael Dillon, and changed the sex on her birth certificate. After this, he qualified as a doctor, and later became a ship's doctor on the British liner *City of Bath*. Nobody, apart from his aunts and a few close friends, knew there had been a change of sex. His story came out in 1958, when an eagle-eyed newspaper reporter noticed a discrepancy in *Burke's* and *Debrett's* peerages. In *Burke's Peerage*, a sister was listed to Sir Robert Dillon, Michael's brother, but in *Debrett's* a brother was listed, Laurence Michael. Both 'brother' and 'sister' had the same date of birth. What could be the explanation?

Newspapers traced Michael Dillon to Philadelphia and challenged him. He was described in *The Daily Sketch* as a pipe-smoking, heavily bearded but rather delicate-looking man. Dillon admitted that he had been registered as a girl at birth but had later developed male characteristics and had eventually registered a change of sex. In the *Sunday Express* Michael's brother was quoted as saying: 'Dr Dillon became my brother some years ago. This is a matter of great delicacy and I don't wish to say too much about it.'

One of the interests of the story was over who should inherit the title. Although Sir Robert, then aged 44, and just over a year older than Michael, was married, he had no children. Only a man could inherit the title. Michael Dillon was quoted as saying that it was not too late for him to become a father, who would then automatically become the heir. In the event, Dillon never became a father. In any case, as he well knew, he was a biologically normal female and could never have fathered children.

After the story came out, Dillon felt that he could no longer carry on as a ship's doctor, and resigned from the liner. Shortly afterwards he became converted to Buddhism and went to India as a Buddhist monk. Having spent some time in southern India he went to Ladakh, where he entered Rizong Monastery as a novice monk. Nobody there, of course, knew his secret. Dillon took the name Lobzang Jivaka and was, it is believed, the very first Englishman to become ordained a Tibetan Buddhist monk. He wrote a book about his experiences as a monk in Ladakh, which was published by Routledge, Kegan Paul under the title *Imji Getsul*, which means 'Tibetan-ordained Buddhist Monk'.

Rizong is one of the most remote, and also among the most strict, of the many monasteries or *gompas* in Ladakh, and Michael Dillon describes graphically what it was like for a middle-aged English doctor to wear the dark red robes and conform to all the practices expected of Buddhist monks. Most monks enter these monasteries when they are children, and never know any other life.

Early in his book Michael Dillon asks how his strange destiny had come about:

How was it that an English doctor came to abandon a promising career, his friends and relatives and the comforts of modern civilization to become, first a *sramenera* [novice] of the Southern School, and then the first Westerner to be a Tibetan-ordained Buddhist monk? To sleep on a wooden bed and later on the floor; to eat with a spoon only and later with the finger or a twig; to wash under a tap and later, if the weather permitted, in an icy mountain stream; to rise with the dawn and later long before it? What was lacking in the teaching he had received in childhood that made him exchange his religion for another?

He answers his own questions by saying that since the age of fifteen he had wanted to find out the truth, and felt that he had finally 'come home' when he discovered Buddhism. He entered Ladakh at a time when the territory was being disputed by India and China, and after several months in the monastery had to leave and was refused re-entry. He died in 1962 in India, supposedly of malnutrition, never having got used to a vegetarian diet.

In many ways Michael Dillon is a sad character, somebody who never found a true rôle in life, either as a woman or as a man. There is no reason to suppose that he was anything but a genetically normal female, and of course he would never have been able to father a child, as he alleged in the *Daily Sketch* story. In that story, Michael Dillon intimated that his sex-change had come about naturally, and that he was the victim of a sex-designation mix-up. This is unlikely, but maybe Dillon felt he had to hide the truth about himself.

There is no evidence that he ever had any sexual experiences, though he did fall in love while at medical school in 1950, just before he qualified. Unfortunately, the affair was unrequited, though Dillon went to the lengths of buying an engagement ring for the girl and telling his landlady he was engaged.

It was after it finally dawned on him that the love affair was one-sided that he became a ship's doctor. Going to sea is, of course, a time-honoured means of escape and also a time-honoured way in which biological women have sought to live as men. There have been several instances of women running away to sea and pretending to be men. But even this didn't take him far enough away, so after his story broke he went to one of the most remote places on earth – Ladakh, in Northern India, where the only road is closed to traffic from June to October every year. In 1986 I visited Dillon's monastery at Ladakh, where one of the older lamas said he remembered the English doctor. Dillon had, it seems, insisted on being treated exactly the same as all the other novice monks, who would have been about twelve years of age.

In his book *Imji Getsul* Michael Dillon writes about how, in spite of all the privations and difficulties, he came to love his life at Rizong and felt that he had truly come home. He writes:

I often felt that I was being pushed along continually towards an unseen goal, and when I wanted to do something that I inwardly knew did not point in that direction, external circumstances would prevent me. But still the purpose eluded me. All I could do was to carry on and wait. If a burning conviction came that I must do a certain thing, I would be able to do it, and it would turn out to be the right thing for continuing the straight line in a forward direction.

At the end of his book Dillon says that he hopes to be

able to return to Ladakh to translate some of the books in the Rizong monastery. But a sad note at the beginning of the book reveals: 'At the time of going to press [summer 1961] the author's application for a permit to re-enter Ladakh has been refused despite all efforts. So at this moment he is debarred from returning to his monastery.'

It seems, from what I have been able to learn of Michael Dillon's life and attitudes, that he completely repudiated the female rôle and adopted an extreme version of the sex stereotype. He wrote in a letter in 1950: 'If women insist on the rights of equality I don't see why they should also demand the privileges of their sex when it suits them. That is always cropping up with the female medical students.' Dillon strenuously denied the female in him, but of course female characteristics continued to exert themselves, and this was probably a factor in his conversion to Buddhism – which is, after all, a non-aggressive and non-competitive way of existence. In other letters, Dillon calls himself a misogynist and a confirmed bachelor, and had no time for feminine matters at all. In the same way, many early male-to-female transsexuals overplayed the feminine rôle to a ridiculous extent. Michael Dillon tried to think of himself as all male, and ruthlessly put down in himself any signs of what he saw as feminine weakness. He saw other transsexuals as 'poor devils', and viewed the coming trend towards female emancipation with horror: 'Man is no longer able to assert himself as rightful lord and master.'

Most present-day female-to-male transsexuals are not like that, thank goodness, yet, curiously, of those I have talked to who have made the change-over in the past few years, none have made as physically complete a transformation as Michael Dillon.

Mark Rees, née Brenda, became famous during 1986 for taking a case to the European court to try to reverse the law which said that no transsexual could change his/her birth certificate unless a genuine mistake had been made at birth. Mark lost the case. Mark, in his mid-forties, is a 'modern' female-to-male transsexual, unlike Michael Dillon, and is certainly not a misogynist or a 'confirmed bachelor', although of course he is unable to marry.

Mark said:

When I was younger I never felt that I was a girl. It wasn't just a question of wanting to play with boys and do boys' things; I actually felt I *was* one. As I grew up, my body became totally abhorrent to me. In the end I felt I had to change my body because it meant that the way other people perceived me was not the way I saw myself. I was treated by others in a way I didn't want to be treated. At school, I refused to wear a petticoat and would wear a collar, tie and blazer even in the hottest weather, simply to cover up my figure. When you feel you are male and you look female, the world seems a very strange place. I couldn't relate to it and it couldn't relate to me.

I was a tomboy as a small child and managed to cope fairly well. It was during puberty that things became acutely painful. Although secondary sexual characteristics were developing – and I couldn't stop them in any way – I always looked ambiguous, and was never comfortable as a girl. When I was in my twenties, girlfriends told me I looked like a drag act as I would always wear men's clothes when I possibly could. The only time I felt normal was when in men's clothes.

In the end, the ambiguity and discomfort became so troublesome that Mark ended up for a time in hospital, having suffered as complete mental breakdown.

Sexually I related to women, but I didn't see myself as lesbian. The thing was, I didn't fit in anywhere and in the end there was nothing for it but to go to a gender-identity clinic and ask to be transformed into a man, as far as possible. Of course I knew that transsexuals were a form of intersex and that the chromosomes could never be changed, and I had to accept that.

I was accepted for treatment straight away and never had any difficulty in convincing doctors of my need to change. The treatment, however, is very unsatisfactory for female-to-male transsexuals. The biggest advantage we have is with the voice – the hormone treatment deepens the voice to sound very convincingly male. Outwardly you can be more convincing as it is quite easy to grow a beard, but of course most of us haven't got male organs. There is still no satisfactory operation in this country to provide a realistic-looking penis, and so far as I know no doctor in Britain is doing the operation. You have to go to America.

The other problem is one that is not due to treatment, and that is height. It seems so unfair that all male-to-female transsexuals are about 6 foot 6, whereas most of us are minute. [Mark says he is 5 foot 4½.] That is okay for a woman – I just wonder what *I've* done to deserve not being taller. But on the whole I have been satisfied with my transformation. When I was still Brenda, people used to look at me in an odd way, as if they couldn't decide which sex I was. Since I began living full time as Mark, I have been completely ignored, which is wonderful. It means I look normal at last. I used to have lots of arguments in the ladies' toilets, where the others would complain that a man had come in.

Mark is a university graduate, with a degree from London University in English Literature. His one regret is that he has been unable to find a job, and, at the time of writing, is still unemployed. 'To be honest, I've almost given up,' he admits. On the question of sex stereotypes, Mark says:

I don't consider that I have fallen into a stereotype. Some transsexuals I know do try to get ridiculously macho, but it doesn't work. I'm certainly not going to swill beer, smoke a pipe or affect any kind of exaggerated masculinity. Sometimes I think that I should know all about cars, now that I'm supposed to be a man, but many of my male friends don't understand mechanical things. I don't feel it is essential at all. I see myself as an ideal person in the middle. Having been a woman, and having grown up, albeit reluctantly, in a woman's world, I find that my sympathies are with women. I find many men boring and pompous. I prefer to listen to women, and feel I know all about them, having been one. Everybody knows about me and I don't try to hide my background as many female-to-male transsexuals do.

Although I am not ridiculously masculine, I am not effeminate either. I just feel that I'm myself at last.

Mark did not seek publicity:

At first my case was going to be heard in confidence. Then the story came out and I decided to brave it. I've been on the 9 o'clock news and countless radio programmes, talking about my right to be recognized as a male. I am in the male rôle, as I see it, and I am certainly more male than female now. At the moment, we don't have an intersex category of humans, and everybody has to be put into boxes, which is ridiculous. The present law benefits nobody.

The government has argued that if birth certificates could be changed, this would allow people to deceive others as to their true sex, but I can't see this happening. How many people really would want to try and pretend they were the other sex?

Mark, like most female-to-male transsexuals in Britain, has had large amounts of male hormone, and also a mastectomy and hysterectomy, but nothing else.

Karl is a biological female, and has lived as a rather masculine lady for most of her life. When aged 50, however, she decided to change over, from Kathleen to Karl, while continuing to live in the same house, and work at the same job.

Karl feels that there are probably just as many female-to-male transsexuals as the other way round, but that they don't talk about it so much, or go for treatment. She reveals:

My only form of treatment so far has been a mastectomy. It didn't change *me* when I had this operation – the most liberating thing I've done in my whole life – but it changed my appearance, and how other people regarded me. For me, the whole matter has always been very simple. From the age of three I felt that I was a boy, and I have always felt I was male. More than that, I *knew* I was a boy. When I had my first bicycle, I insisted on having a T-bar, and would not ride a girl's bike. As a child, it troubled me that my parents didn't see me as a boy. Why didn't they see that?, I used to ask myself.

It became clear to me early in life that I was not ever going to fit into a female world. By the age of fourteen I had all the physical attributes of a girl and knew then that I would come up against enormous obstacles. I was never attracted to boys, and knew that the only relationship I could ever have was with a woman – not as a lesbian, but as a husband.

In those days, of course, it was never talked about, and I felt very sad and disturbed. There was nobody for me to confide in, nobody I could go to for help. I didn't even know what kind of help I wanted. I knew that I wanted to be married and to father children, but of course I also knew that was impossible. So how best to live my life?

I struggled on as best I could until I was 46, when I met an understanding doctor. For all those years before that I had lived as a female, although I never wore anything but trousers out of work. I found that if I wore a collar and tie and blazer, nobody looked at me in a peculiar way. Now I am 55, and have five years to go before retirement in my job in the health service.

I decided to make a permanent change on my fiftieth birthday. I had the mastectomy, and took the decision to wear trousers and men's clothes all the time, even to work. When people come into the office, they expect to see a woman, but just treat me and regard me as a man.

Karl says he cannot tell whether he now feels like a man.

What does being a man feel like? Could any man answer that question? If I had had a chance to marry and settle down as a man, living an ordinary male life, I might be able to answer that question. All I know is that for the first time in my life I feel right. I haven't got any male bulges, but that is a minor problem. The main thing is, I haven't got to live as a woman any more. It seems to me that I was meant to be male, but that something went wrong en route. It can't be environmental, as my parents didn't particularly wish for a boy, or bring me up as one.

The only explanation of the condition that makes sense to me is that the programming starts before birth and then continues, against all the odds. I have never felt any differently but I saw early on that I would have no real place in the world because I was different from other people. I just know what I should have been, but fate decreed that I was not.

Karl doesn't feel that psychiatric counselling helps at all. 'I dispute the value of it,' he told me:

For most women, to have a mastectomy is a major emotional trauma, but for me it actually removed the trauma, and I didn't need any counselling from anybody to tell me that. My doctor told me that my sense of humour about the situation saved me. I have certainly never regretted having the mastectomy, although I could never have had such a operation during my father's lifetime. He could never have accepted the idea of mutilating a perfect body.

As it was, I had a wonderful job done and it cost just £100. My private insurance scheme paid for the lot, and it was literally and symbolically a huge weight off my chest. Unfortunately, as luck would have it, I was particularly well endowed up there, though I am small everywhere else. [Like many female-to-male transsexuals, Karl is not tall – just over 5 foot 4.]

To add to the irony, a lot of us are small. When I started to

wear men's clothes all the time the word went round that I'd
had a sex-change operation. But the mastectomy is all I've had.
It would be a major problem using public conveniences, so I
just never do. Another problem is that I love dancing, but if I go
dancing as a man, my partner might find out that I'm not a real
man. If she wants more, I can't provide it. So there are
difficulties, but they are mainly on the practical level. People
have never found any problems in relating to me as a man, the
ones who have known me all along, probably because I was
never a feminine woman. I do identify very much with Radclyffe Hall. If she'd been able to have a sex change, she would
have made a fantastic man. Radclyffe Hall had problems in
being faithful to one partner, and was in that sense a playboy.

I feel that I'm fortunate in that I work in a woman's world.
Most of my colleagues in the office are female and I can feel
more masculine in their company. I know that my gender is
masculine but that the biology can never be changed. I can't
help feeling rather bitter at times because there is nothing I
would have loved more than to marry as a man, have children
and be a proper husband and father. It doesn't really make any
difference that I haven't had a 'proper' sex change, because the
artificial plumbing doesn't really work and, anyway, it still
wouldn't make me any more of a man than I am already.

The main thing I'm grateful for is that my life is now
workable, and my outward appearance conforms to my inner
image of myself. When I had to wear a skirt, it seemed as if I
changed sex four times a day, as I would take it off the minute I
came home from work.

Stephen, who lives in Manchester, is in his early thirties and changed over at the age of twenty:

From the age of three or four, I knew I wasn't happy being a
girl. I never liked wearing skirts and identified far more with
my two younger brothers than my two older sisters. In every
way I was the odd one out in the family, and was never able to
come to terms with myself. It wasn't that I thought I was a boy. I
knew I was a girl, but I also knew that I didn't want to be a girl.

At secondary school I was never able to identify with the
other girls, but I was athletic and sporty and quite popular, the
team-captain type. I never ever had a boyfriend, or was
attracted to boys, but I did have crushes on other girls. That
made me decide that I must be lesbian.

Yet even that didn't seem to go far enough. When I was
seventeen I read an article in a woman's magazine about a

145

female-to-male transsexual, and then it all became clear. Immediately I identified with that person and everything clicked. At the time I was deputy head girl at school and cricket captain, but I went to pieces and had three months off school. I knew what I was, but what the hell was I going to do about it?

Anyway, I left school and went to teacher-training college, where I was unable to complete the course. By this time I'd had my first lesbian experience and I read everything I could about how to change sex. Somehow, I knew I wasn't gay. I couldn't relate to other gay people and didn't fancy sex with women. Lesbians wanted me to be a woman, whereas I wanted to be a man. After drifting in and out of the gay world, I eventually joined a radical lesbian collective and after a year knew beyond all possible doubt that my fundamental problem was that I wanted to be a bloke.

At one of the gay bars Stephen frequented at the time a woman came up to him and said that a sex change was what he really wanted. So, at the age of nineteen-and-a-half, Stephen started to have male hormone treatment.

So I never became a woman. I had quite a reasonable job as a technician at a polytechnic and I was able to keep this on throughout the change. I became 'Mr' and carried on with the hormone treatment. I had to wait five years for surgery, which was tedious, but I later went to university as Stephen, with the university authorities knowing my background.

What happens on male hormone is that within two months your periods stop and after six to nine months your voice breaks. After a year, there is beard growth. That is the average, although everybody varies in their response to hormones. My beard is my pride and joy, and became a necessity. At the age of 26 I shaved off my beard and went into a pub, where they refused to serve me as they said I was under age. The beard does help you to look more masculine and convincing. As I am only 5 foot 2, looking like a 'real' man has its problems. The extra height would have added an enormous amount of credibility. As I am physically very slight as well, I can't help looking boyish and much younger than I am.

Eventually I had a mastectomy and hysterectomy. The mastectomy meant that I no longer had to bind my breasts – the male hormone doesn't alter those. I found before I had the hysterectomy that every time I stopped taking the massive doses of male hormone I would get breakthrough bleeding and gynaecological problems. So far I haven't had a phalloplasty, though I have met some people who have. The surgery is appalling, and you can get rejection, as with any graft.

I understand that techniques advanced during the Vietnam war but there are grave disadvantages and so far I haven't felt the necessity to go ahead. I am lucky enough to have a girlfriend – the same one for the past eight years – and we manage to have an adequate sex life. If, at the end of the day, I could be granted 95 per cent success with a phalloplasty, I would go ahead. But at the moment it seems as though it's playing with fire.

One guy I know is saving up the $25,000 needed to have the operation in America, but at the end of the day it's still only cosmetic.

Stephen now lives in a large house with eight other people and his girlfriend Sarah, a nurse. He said:

The question of whether we live in a predominantly man's world crops up over and over again here. Although I am living as a man, I haven't acquired the technical or electrical skills that most lads grow up with. I have got physics A-level, but most of the 'masculine' skills I've had to learn much later. I feel I now have both female and male skills, but I've noticed that there is a sharp division of labour in this house, even though we all try to be liberal. On the whole, the women do cooking and shopping while the men mend cars. It's interesting that, though we are all graduates and consider ourselves unstereotyped, the pre-ordained rôles still seem to come out.

At the moment I am self-employed, but my last job was as a finance manager in an all-women office. I was living and working as a man, and the women found me quite surprising. They said, 'You're not like the other men – you actually listen to us.' Of course, none of them knew I was a transsexual. I feel that the old-time transsexuals did encourage stereotypes, but that the modern ones don't. I try to lead as normal a life as possible without being over-masculine. I do loads of sport and run a scout group. I have to be careful on camps so that nobody finds out about me. I've discovered that when people do find out, there is trouble. I have been sacked from one job, and I have discovered that if people know you are a transsexual it can be difficult to get promotion. You are somehow considered unreliable.

I think it is very difficult to progress in normal-type jobs and certainly I would be out of scouting if anybody knew about me. My only real problem in life is that Sarah and I can't have children. We would both like them, and if anything ever breaks up our relationship, this will be it. We have got to the stage of fixing an appointment with an adoption agency, though I can't say whether we will get anywhere.

Stephen is now a property developer. He claims that in spite of the problems he faces the difference in living as a man is 'unbelievable'.

Before the age of nineteen, life was a continuous really bad nightmare. The further I get removed from my childhood and adolescence, the more like a bad dream it becomes. I feel as if I've never had a childhood. It's as if the past wasn't real. Being a man is where I belong, and I simply can't imagine being anything else.

It's often said that sex-change people are narcissistic, but the irony is that you are far more conscious of yourself before the sex change. You are aware of being so continually unhappy. Now I feel normal, like everybody else, even if, from a fully functional point of view, I'm not actually normal.

Richard, in his early thirties, works in a computer company where he had a very public change of sex, stopping work as a woman just before a holiday and returning a few weeks later as a man. This sounds bizarre, but for Richard it was the path to feeling right.

He says:

I was the eldest of four children, and aware that something was wrong with me as far back as I can remember. I didn't exactly know what I wanted, but I was very confused about myself. My parents may have wanted a boy, I don't know, but I'm sure that is not the explanation. I always rebelled if ever I had to put on a dress, and when I was taken to ballet lessons it was the most total disaster.

I refused to wear anything but wellingtons at my ballet lessons, which didn't exactly make me popular with the teacher. But mainly things weren't too difficult up to adolescence because I could quite happily be a tomboy. I had no doubt as a child that I would grow up to be a boy, and that things would right themselves somehow. On my first day at school, the teachers gave me a pink sticker, and I can remember to this day thinking they had made a ridiculous mistake. 'Don't they know I'm a boy?' I can remember asking myself.

It was with adolescence that the problems really started. Everybody expected that I would grow out of my tomboyish ways and settle down as a teenage girl. But I never did. I made a fuss about wanting to do woodwork instead of cookery, and I hated doing girls' sports, such as netball. At secondary school the problems all intensified. I felt so completely wrong as a girl that I simply couldn't stand it. Then when I was about thirteen or fourteen I read in the *Daily Telegraph* about somebody who had changed sex and become a man, and immediately I knew that was what I had to do.

I forced myself at school to become an extrovert and became a rebel. I was put into the thickies' class and never expected to get any O-levels, but eventually I made it to university. When I was in the sixth form, life just became impossible. I kept falling in love with girls, yet couldn't see myself as a lesbian. It was as if girls were the opposite, not the same, sex. I simply can't describe how I felt when my body changed to that of a girl and there was no longer any mistaking my sex. I just cringed every time I saw myself in the mirror. The worst thing was that I kept getting pressure to behave in a more feminine way, and to look more feminine. Everybody started reacting to me as a girl, and this was really terrible. I knew they had got hold of the wrong end of the stick about me.

I didn't talk to anybody about it, but that newspaper article gave me a speck of hope which kept me going.

Richard got a job and said he got to the point of living two lives, the outward one and the real one inside his head. Whenever possible he would dress as a man, and this induced hostility in other people. 'I felt so much pressure to conform,' he said. 'But as the years went by, things got worse and worse until eventually, at the age of 26, I could stand it no longer, and set about changing my sex to live permanently as a man.'

Richard later went to university to read geography, and became a Christian. It was after university that he decided to seek treatment, and went to a gender-identity clinic.

I knew they existed, and thought they would be the only places that could help me. I moved to London and got a job as a trainee computer-programmer and had to wear a skirt. I felt just like a man in drag and as soon as I got home I would take off all my female clothes and put on men's ones instead. Then I could be me. My family thought I was lesbian, and didn't understand the real nature of my problem.

When I eventually did tell them, it took them ages to come

round and accept the situation. Once I had made up my mind, I planned and prepared how I would change over. I had to tell my manager at work, then I told my own team. It was very difficult, changing over so publicly, but I did keep my job. At work I was looked at more closely, and some people became suspicious, but everybody made a tremendous effort.

I found the gender-identity clinic at Guy's Hospital – which has now closed down, I believe – very sympathetic and helpful. At first the psychiatrist wouldn't let me have treatment but later referred me for testosterone injections. I've had a mastectomy but have still got female internal organs. If ever I decided to have a phalloplasty, I think I would have to go to America. Hardly anything is available here, and certainly not on the NHS.

It does matter a lot to me to be as normal a male as possible. I know the constructed penis is only cosmetic, but as long as it looks all right and performs reasonably well, I'll be satisfied. I don't accept that transsexualism is a psychological disorder. If it was, then people could be treated with psychology, but they can't. Surgery and hormones are the only answer. Now that I am a man – or at least am living full-time as one – I am so much more peaceful in myself, and I have better friendships. I am more in harmony with the external world.

Richard feels that we live in a man's world and that male egos are more fragile than those of women:

Most men try to exert their power and influence, and you are more vulnerable as a woman. I can't say whether the testosterone has altered my personality, but I have definitely become physically stronger since taking it. One thing that works to my advantage is that I have very close friendships with women. Lots of men at work who don't know about me envy how well I get on with women, and how much I seem to understand them. I've noticed that lots of men can't talk properly to women at all.

I have also got a lot of close male friends, and in every way life has improved since I began treatment. There are people who say that surgery doesn't make any difference, but it does. All the people I know who have had medical treatment for transsexuality have improved in themselves as a result. I don't think there is any way that I could ever have come to terms with having a female body.

It's true that the sexes are still very far apart. Perhaps transsexuals can help to bring them together. This hasn't happened in the past, I know, as most transsexuals want to forget they were ever members of the other sex, but we are the only people who have direct experience of both sides.

Tim, a writer in his early forties, is one of the few female-to-male transsexuals in Britain to have a phalloplasty. At the time of writing he has already had six operations, but will need at least one more before the construction of an artificial penis is considered complete. He says:

I know many female-to-male transsexuals don't have the phalloplasty, but for me there was no way I would have wanted to go through with it all unless I could have reasonably authentic-looking male organs. For me, there were three considerations to bear in mind: sexual function, appearance and sensation, not necessarily in that order.

The operations are very tough, as a pedicle flap has to be raised on the abdomen, and construction of a male-type urethra is very difficult indeed. Your need has to be as great as mine otherwise you would never go through with it.

For the past eighteen months, Tim says he has done little but have operations and then spend time recovering. It takes an average of three to four weeks to recover from each visit to the surgeon. Tim, who finally decided to change over at the age of 35, says he spent a great deal of time sussing out surgeons, until he found one who would do the operations sensitively and carefully, leaving no scars, or as few as possible. 'I've seen some terrible jobs,' he said. 'I know from my researches that there is no need for huge scars. This was very important when I had my mastectomy.'

Tim had all of his operations on the NHS and says that, contrary to common belief, phalloplasty is available under the health service in Britain. 'There was no way I would have considered a sex change without the phalloplasty,' he said.

My problems wouldn't have been solved otherwise. I had to get my body as right as possible. Now I can go into a man's changing room, strip off, and I look like all the other men. Obviously I can't ejaculate, and anybody who had intimate contact with me would soon realize there was something different. But to the superficial eye, the operation is completely successful.

Tim's operations were carried out by a new micro-surgery technique, and in his view procedures are improving all the time. 'Obviously surgeons can't reproduce erectile tissue,' he said. 'But in all other respects, the end result can be very impressive. It depends very much on the surgeon.' Tim's final operation will be to enable an implant to be inserted which will give him an erection and make sexual intercourse possible. There are techniques for permanent implants, but mine will be removable,' he said. 'It doesn't hurt at all to put on, and is in fact no more trouble than a condom.'

The operation for artificial testes was made by sewing the labia majora together to form a scrotum, and the 'testicles' are silicon implants. 'This was quite a simple operation compared to construction of the penis,' Tim claims.

Tim – who, like many female-to-male transsexuals, does not want personal publicity – said that he only identified his condition at the age of 29:

Obviously I always knew I wanted to be a boy, and I suffered agonies during puberty, because I saw my body changing into a shape that, for me, was quite wrong. It seemed to me that I was terribly deformed.

Now, looking back, I see transsexuality as a physical rather than a psychological thing. I feel far closer to physically disabled people than to those with a sexual problem. Once I realized that I could not identify with my body, I knew I had to put it right. My body was all wrong and in the end I could not live with it.

I have tried hard not to be a chauvinist, or to overdo the masculinity, and have a strong affinity with women's liberation. In the end I had to ask myself the ultimate question: if we lived in a society where there were no sex stereotypes, and where a particular shape of body did not predispose you to a rôle, would I still want to change? The answer was yes. It was as deep as that.

For me, it wasn't enough just to dress as a man, I had to *be* one, as far as was humanly possible. I had to have a proper relationship with my own body, and so there was an essential need for the phalloplasty.

It is hard for a non-transsexual to understand, but there is terrible pain in having what you consider the wrong bits attached. After my first operation I was on a high for weeks and genuinely felt as if I had been reborn.

When I first began living as a man I expected to feel very insecure, but I never did. [Like many female-to-male transsexuals, Tim is not tall – 5 foot 4½.] It is ironic that we are all so short, and the male-to-female transsexuals seem to be extremely tall. But before I finally decided to change over, I spent a lot of time studying men's heights, and noticed that lots were around my height. So it hasn't mattered at all. I used to walk down the street and notice how many men who were passing by were taller than me, and not all that many were. Now I have virtually completed my change-over, I don't feel short at all.

Tim is living in a husband-and-wife relationship with his long-term girlfriend, and is both a vegetarian and a Buddhist.

'The story of Michael Dillon interests me a lot,' he said. 'I think that we have made some progress in behaviour since those days, as most of us don't feel the need to act ridiculously masculine. Of course Dillon, being a pioneer, had no rôle models at all.'

CHAPTER 8

Transsexuals, homosexuals and transvestites

In Pattaya Beach in Thailand, the resort which was originally used by American GIs during the Vietnam War, one can see a very impressive travesty show. Beautiful young men come on and dance and sing and do 'turns'. As one watches, the question arises, and nags at one with increasing urgency: can they really be men? For as well as being facially beautiful, many of them have well-developed female breasts, which they are only too anxious to show off, and there are no signs of any male organs at all. The audience is assured that, contrary to what you might think, the cast is entirely male. Mainly these men are homosexual, and one is informed that several, though not all, have had 'the operation'.

Many men dress up as women in order to entertain. The device is as old as entertainment itself. All of Shakespeare's female characters, it must be remembered, were played by boys, which is why so many are androgynous, or downright boyish. Then there is the traditional pantomime dame. Comedians such as Barry Humphries and Danny la Rue have created enduring 'female' characters of a grotesque type. Dame Edna Everage, 'housewife superstar', is perhaps the most grotesque of all. After April Ashley's short career as a merchant seaman ended, but before she had her operation, she became a member of a famous drag troupe at Le Carrousel in Paris. In her memoirs, she gives a racy account of life behind the scenes at this nightclub and tells us that Cochinelle, the star of the show, later had a sex-change operation, and married her boyfriend in a very public ceremony at Notre-Dame.

Drag acts have stood the test of time and are enduringly

popular. Hinge and Bracket are one of the few drag double-acts and comedians such as Benny Hill and the Two Ronnies (Barker and Corbett) are also fond of appearing in drag.

In the minds of the public at large, transvestites, homosexuals and transsexuals are all examples of much the same thing, with transsexuality being the most extreme version. They all belong, in popular imagination, to that twilight world of the kinky, the effeminate, or perhaps the pantomime. A large part of the humour in the routines of Danny la Rue, Barry Humphries and Hinge and Bracket lies in the fact that we know they are men. We know they are not real. When you meet Danny la Rue or Barry Humphries out of drag, they don't look in the least like women. Yet they become them, or absurd versions of them, during their stage and television shows. Are homosexuals, transvestites and transsexuals really just a continuum, or are there major differences which distinguish the three groups?

There are overlaps, of course, but as this chapter will try to show, there are also enormous differences – differences which have become rather blurred by the world of entertainment. Some men who dress in drag for comedy purposes are homosexual and some are not. Barry Humphries is clearly heterosexual, and when not in drag is not effeminate in the least. Neither he nor Danny la Rue can be termed transvestites, as they dress up purely to entertain. The men parading at Pattaya Beach, by contrast, are probably all three – homosexuals, transvestites and transsexuals. They have all taken hormone treatment, and cannot change back into 'real' men. Similarly, many of the artistes at Le Carrousel were on female hormones, and many were waiting for the operation; indeed, they were appearing at the nightclub in order to raise money for the purpose.

So it is not surprising that the public mixes the three groups up. Also, most psychology textbooks dealing with sexual deviation tend to lump the three conditions together, or at least try to show that they have a common cause, either biological or environmental.

Homosexuality is probably the most prevalent of the

three conditions. There are no reliable statistics to say just how many men have had a homosexual experience in their lives, but some authorities put it as high as 30 per cent. Countless men are bisexual. Bisexuality is very common indeed, and appears to be on the increase. For many years now, gays have been pleading for treatment as normal individuals whose sexual proclivities should not be a matter for concern or discrimination. They have achieved this up to a point, but many 'straight' people are still nervous about and wary of known homosexuals. But homosexuals themselves are not by any means all cast in the same mould. Some, such as Quentin Crisp, are very effeminate and like to wear make-up and nail varnish. Some of these may like to dress occasionally as women, or wear clothes which make it hard to tell which sex they are supposed to be. Then there is the 'scene' – a form of dress and appearance by which gays can recognize each other. There are also gay men who do not look or act differently from heterosexual men. But whatever the outward signs, none of these men would ever want to be women, even though on occasion they may be referred to as 'she'. Clearly, all homosexuals embody the feminine principle to some extent – large numbers are found in the performing arts, and in other areas of the creative arts, as painters, poets, sculptors and writers. They tend, on the whole, to be more creative and imaginative then many heterosexual men. Some homosexual men have sex-change operations. But those who have the operation will be people who have from their earliest years regarded themselves as women. By far the great majority of homosexual men glory in their male organs, and would never want to lose them. Similarly, most homosexual women – lesbians – would not want to turn into men. They enjoy their own sexual identity but prefer to relate sexually to members of their own gender. The thought of changing over would not be acceptable to them.

Though many male homosexuals act in a limp, effeminate manner, this does not mean they want to be women. Indeed, effeminate behaviour is most emphatically not womanly behaviour – it is always obviously a man being camp. Similarly, a female homosexual, however butch, does not behave like a man. There are subtle differences which are difficult to describe but can be spotted instantly and accurately, by anyone. Homosexuals enjoy remaining in their original sex. It is just that, for some reason still not understood, they prefer to liaise sexually, and in a way which will not be procreative, with members of their own sex.

Some transsexuals become homosexual on the way to sorting themselves out. For many, the step of accepting themselves as transsexuals is a difficult one to take; seeing themselves as homosexual seems more 'normal'. Moreover, some doctors and psychiatrists in the past have tried to persuade transsexuals to see themselves as gay rather than straight, and leave it there. By and large, however, homosexuals are people who are quite happy to remain in their original sex, and this is in fact a source of pleasure to them. They would not want to be any different.

Transvestites are people who like to dress in the clothes of the opposite sex. They are in some ways closer to transsexuals, who also cross-dress, but most transvestite men would never want to *be* women. They dress in women's clothes for the purposes of sexual arousal, and this arousal comes from the sure and certain knowledge that underneath the petticoats, knickers and suspender belts they are truly and unequivocally male. Indeed, most of them will have huge erections underneath the female clothes, and it is to provoke this erection that the clothes are put on in the first place. True transsexuals never become sexually aroused by wearing women's clothes and most do not even want to become aroused. For the average pre-operative transsexual, sexual arousal is a nuisance, reminding him that he is of the sex he does not want to be. When referring to transvestites, I am using the male gender – not as a pseudo-generic term, but because all transvestites are male. True, some women dress in men's clothes, even some women who are not transsexual. But it is *never* for the purposes of sexual arousal. Women who wear men's clothes do it because, for them, it feels right, or is appropriate to the occasion. Princess Diana has on occasion worn a man's dinner-jacket to a pop concert, which everybody applauded, but it would not be considered acceptable for Prince Charles to wear an off-the-shoulder sequinned gown.

Transvestites are usually, though not exclusively, heterosexual men who have an unusual proclivity. I am not talking here about entertainers, but men who cross-dress in secret and in private, or who belong to special clubs where this is done. There have been many theories about what makes a man a transvestite, but so far nobody has offered one which is truly convincing.

The true transsexual is distinguished from these two groups by the fact that he wants to dress in female clothes all the time, not just occasionally for the purposes of sexual arousal. The reason he does this is because he actually believes he is a woman, and by wearing female clothes he puts his inner and outer existences into harmony. Many transsexuals, both male and female, cross-dress in secret at first; at this stage they are not really sure why they do it. They know it feels right to them but they also know that society says it is wrong. Gradually, however, they gain enough self-confidence to appear in public in the clothes of the 'correct' sex, as they see it, and some may go on to do this all the time, like Karl, whose story was told in the previous chapter, or Melanie Jane. Once they are cross-dressing on an everyday basis, in their own eyes they become real men and women, though they may still retain organs of their original sex.

Above all, transsexuals are distinct from homosexuals and transvestites because they want to be permanently rid of their original sex organs. Nothing will satisfy them until this is done, and just dressing up is usually not enough. Moreover, most transsexuals are not very interested in leading active sex lives, and by far the great majority are asexual. Some have partners, and some manage to have sexual relationships, but sex usually plays a very minor rôle in their lives. Transsexuals do not have the operation in order to pursue an active sex life, but so that they can feel at peace with themselves.

In his book *The Transsexual Experiment* Robert Stoller makes a very clear distinction between transsexuals and transvestites. The transvestite, he says, has a fetishistic urge to dress in women's clothes and it is the actual dressing-up which produces a much-longed-for erection. The sexual act of cross-dressing focuses attention on the male genitals, and a transvestite would certainly not consider himself in any way a woman trapped in a man's body. He is quite the opposite, more than pleased to be a fully functioning, potent male. Also, his cross-dressing is intermittent, not an everyday practice. He cannot, according to Stoller, hide for very long the fact that he is a man dressed in women's clothes. The transsexual, however does not have an intermittent desire to dress as a woman; and while dressed as such he will do everything possible to ensure that the secret does not come out. The transsexual, says Stoller, has no difficulty in passing full-time as a woman, and indeed, he adds, many adolescent pre-operative transsexuals manage to pass completely successfully as women at their first attempt.

Many transsexuals find it quite difficult to be properly masculine, but the transvestite has no such problem. Transvestites, according to Stoller, have no desire to be women, even unconsciously. He postulates that they behave as they do perhaps because of some childhood incident: a woman acted threateningly, leaving for ever after the unconscious desire to pay this woman back. That, at any rate, is Stoller's theory. When a beautiful boy is born to a beautiful woman, says Stoller, there may be a danger of homosexuality, but never of transvestism. The fetish has a quite different dynamic. But transsexuals are not men who are more beautiful and more womanly-looking than average. Their conviction of being female has nothing whatever to do with their original physical appearance, and is quite separate from it.

Some men like to wear women's clothes for the sensation it gives them of being different, and for the excitement, but would always want to remain men. One such is John Colvin, who gave an account of his transvestism in *The Guardian* in January 1986. His story was accompanied by a picture of him looking soulful and odd in a sleeveless drop-waist print summer dress.

He wrote:

I first had the idea I wanted to wear dresses in public (as well as private) just over a year ago, but it took me a full year to summon up the courage actually to do so. Of course I felt supported by the fact that some other men have started to wear dresses publicly. However, such men remain very much in a minority and I have yet to find out what, for them, such dressing is all about.

For myself, I am very clear that I am not interested in cross-dressing; that is, dressing like a woman. Rather, for me, I am wearing the dress *as a man* and am therefore making a statement about my masculinity . . . In particular, wearing my dresses gives me feelings of sensuality toward my body, together with feelings of vulnerability, which I am not able otherwise to experience so directly. Equally important to me is the fact that I move very differently in a dress. My movements feel more fluid, and I am able to adopt postures and gestures which are completely beyond the normal range when wearing trousers or shorts.

What about transvestism, though? According to one survey, there are now a quarter of a million transvestites in the UK. In which case a man wearing a dress is hardly new. However, I think there is a difference between my motives and those of most of the others. Most men dress to look like women – not only do they wear women's clothes, including underclothes, but also wigs and make-up to achieve a full effect. And approximately one per cent of men will go further – they actually feel that they really are women and in many cases are able to seek a sex-change operation. Now, clearly, by wearing a dress I am to some extent embracing both these themes – the desire in each case to experience aspects of femininity. However I am also asserting that I do not wish to compromise those aspects of my masculinity which I value and indeed that I wish to remain a man and be seen as a man, while bringing together valued aspects of both masculinity and femininity into an appropriate image.

Clearly, John Colvin is not a transsexual. He is a man who wishes to remain a man but who experiences a need to get in touch with the more feminine aspects of himself. In order to do this he feels he has to wear a more feminine type of garment than usual. He says later in the same article that he wants to be seen as a Real Man, and hopes that society's moves towards greater androgyny and freedom in dress may point the way to a great understanding between the sexes.

John Colvin cannot be considered a 'true' transvestite, either, as he does not appear to gain sexual satisfaction by wearing dresses. He seems interested only in making some sort of political statement about the polarization between the sexes, and how he is trying to alter this.

'Geraldine', by contrast, is a true transvestite and his (her?) story is told in a book written by his landlady, Monica Jay. Monica, now in her sixties, has had a traumatic life. Both her parents perished at the Auschwitz concentration camp. Later she came to England and married, but the marriage was not happy. In due course she divorced her husband and set up a boarding house, which is how she came to meet Gerald, a suave, educated, sophisticated, upper-class man of the type she had always longed to meet. Some time after Gerald moved into her house they had an affair, and for the first time Monica felt she awoke sexually – was desired, and also felt desire. But there was something peculiar about Gerald: he liked to dress in women's clothes. He told Monica that was why his marriage had broken up, and why he had come to live, incongruously as it seemed at first, in a rooming house.

Monica Jay was shocked at first, and in her book, *Geraldine – For the Love of a Transvestite*, describes what happened to Gerald when he was dressed up as a woman. In his case, dressing up included the whole works – false breasts, tightly laced corselette, shaven body, French knickers, hip padding. Monica says:

When he told me I thought it would be just like an actor dressing up in costume. But it wasn't. His whole personality changed. It really was a different person standing there in front of me. I was frightened. I thought: this is ridiculous. There is a limit. On the other hand, I was now in love with him, and I knew he was inside there somewhere.

After Gerald eventually left Monica's house for a job abroad, and the affair came to an end, she became interested in transvestites and began working as a counsellor to help them. She now feels she understands transvestites, and knows what the condition is all about. In her view:

Most transvestites are just normal blokes who want to put on a woman's dress to relax and that's about it . . . Transvestism is something people don't want to touch. They joke about it. It makes them feel uneasy. When a woman dresses as a man she takes on his highest status. We call it fashion. But the other way round is demeaning and perverted.

Most transvestites don't want to be 'cured'. They enjoy it too much. I was talking to an intelligent man about it the other day. He had just lost his wife and family because of his cross-dressing. But he told me, 'If they gave me a pill that would cure it right now, I wouldn't swallow it.' And he was no fool.

Most wives and partners are horrified and uncomprehending when they discover that their men want to dress up in women's clothes from time to time. They are especially disconcerted when they find that the clothes in question are usually of an extremely fetishistic nature: six-inch heels, cruelly-laced corsets and exaggerated bras – the kind of 'glamour' clothes some men try to persuade their wives to wear in the privacy of the bedroom. Transvestism can be regarded as exhibitionistic and fetishistic but, beyond that, it is usually quite harmless and one sometimes wonders what all the fuss is about. Transvestities do not normally become violent and aggressive when in women's clothes – it's just something they seem to have to get out of their system from time to time.

An article in a woman's magazine illustrates how some wives can over-react to something which really should not make any difference to a marital partnership. The anonymous wife in the story writes:

He had make-up smeared all over his face and he looked absolutely grotesque. I went crazy. I remember screaming at him: 'What are you doing? For God's sake take those things off . . .'

He calmed me down and started laughing. He said, 'Oh come on. What are you making a fuss about?'

The husband promised never to do it again and kept to his promise until the couple's daughter had been born and was about a year old. The wife continues:

It was then that I noticed a holdall on top of the wardrobe. I pulled it down – and nearly went mad.

It was full of the most garish women's clothes you could ever imagine. There were mini-skirts spangled with sequins, revealing evening dresses, sexy black underwear and nighties. There were false boobs, blonde and red wigs, strappy, high-heeled shoes and even handbags. I have never seen such outrageous things – things that few ordinary women would ever want to wear.

I stared at them feeling completely numb. I suppose what had happened before was still in my mind, and although Rick had promised me then that he was only playing games, I knew this was different.

I felt physically sick. What had happened to my husband? This wasn't the man I had married. This wasn't a man. He must be some kind of pervert, dressing up in clothes like this. It was disgusting, obscene, kinky . . . I found myself mouthing words I didn't even know I knew as, mechanically, I tidied up the house and began to get supper . . .

To say that my life had been completely shattered is no exaggeration. Everything had suddenly turned upside down. To me it was worse than knowing my husband had died. He was still here, but changed into something evil. I couldn't bear to have him touch me any more or watch him playing with our daughter. When he tried to kiss me as he went off to work, I shrank away.

When he had gone, I used to pretend I didn't have a husband . . . Once I saw him, primping and preening in front of the mirror as he put make-up on. I shouted, 'You're evil. You're disgusting!'

In time, she says, she learned to live with it and resume a normal married life with her husband. 'I try to understand what he does and I have learned to live with it now. But accept it? I never will.'

On one level it could be said that for men homosexuality, transvestism and transsexualism are a matter of degree, in that they all reveal a female side of the personality emerging. Everybody possesses both male and female attributes, physically as well as mentally and emotionally. This is why men have nipples, which serve no purpose at all, and women have clitorises, which, again, have no biological function. Many of us, however, do not acknowledge our 'other' side. Gays and transvestites acknowledge it publicly but whereas many gays are recognizable, and transvestites are also recognizable when cross-dressed, transsexuals usually look exactly the same as other straight men. When cross-dressed, they usually look like normal women.

Homosexuality also has something in common with transsexualism in that it appears to be biologically based. It is completely cross-cultural and does not appear to be affected by environmental influences. Gay men are gay in their bones: it is something deep within them, almost as if they were wired up differently from straight men. Homosexuality does not seem to be something they have consciously learned or tried to acquire but a trait which emerges naturally, sooner or later. Gayness is embedded deep in the personality, and nothing will shift it. Male homosexuals may decide not to practise, but they will still be gay in other respects. A gay man can never be 'cured', and few would ever want to be. They basically like being as they are.

Malcolm J. MacCullough, writing in the *British Journal of Sexual Medicine* for February 1980, advances a biochemical theory for homosexuality. He postulates that male homosexuality may be caused by a female-differentiated brain, that is, one in which the right amount of masculinizing androgens were not present at the critical time, pre-birth. For lesbians, the opposite case would apply, with too few feminizing oestrogens being present. Mac-Cullough says:

The animal and human data both support the hypothesis that both male and female primary homosexuality may be biochemically determined by *in utero* conditions: specifically that pre-natal exposure to abnormal levels of sex hormones may control brain differentiation and the direction of sexual choice in adult life.

Whether this is true or not, it is the case that male homosexuals, in common with transsexuals, usually have completely normal and average amounts of male hormone circulating in their systems. The same is true of lesbians and female-to-male transsexuals.

The biochemical view of homosexuality and transsexualism suggests that such people cannot help their orientation and proclivities. This is certainly the more modern view and is starting to replace the old, post-natal explanation which centred on blaming the mother for turning the son into a homosexual, transvestite or transsexual, or the daughter into a lesbian.

Although homosexuality, transvestism and transsexuality are to some extent interlinked, in that they are all conditions not consciously chosen or sought, and all are considered to constitute, to some extent, aberrations from the norm, they are all very different in their outcome and manifestations. Those of a homosexual or transvestite inclination are usually sexually active, and their sex lives are extremely important to them. Also, the conditions do not normally cause a high level of unhappiness, except perhaps to near relatives such as parents or spouses.

Transsexuality, by contrast, generally causes great, sometimes unbearable, unhappiness for the sufferer, and brings much confusion and concern. Though homosexuals and transvestites would not usually want to be cured, and are more than happy to remain as they are, the average transsexual would do anything to feel normal, and not to have the unalterable conviction that his or her body must be altered, and that a happy life can only be lived in a gender other than the biological one. Most transsexuals would ask nothing more from life than to be able to accept themselves in their original gender, and live as their biology dictates. But they cannot do this. Most transsexuals are deeply unhappy about their duality. They feel that they do not belong anywhere, that the world is not relevant to them, and that they can never fall in love or have the kind of relationships they imagine other people enjoy. They wonder what they can do to make themselves feel all right, and they soon discover that it is not enough to dress occasionally in the clothes of the opposite sex, or to have sexual relations with members of their own sex.

Unlike transvestites and female impersonators, true transsexuals do not normally choose glamorous feminine clothes – rather the reverse; they tend to go for garments which are quiet and understated, the more understated and unlikely to be noticed the better. When Judy Cousins

165

was living as a woman, but before she had her operation, she would often dress in women's clothes, but would always choose quiet, unremarkable outfits. The very last thing she wanted was for people to think she was a man in drag. A great many other transsexuals I have met feel the same, and I have yet to meet one who dresses like Danny la Rue or Dame Edna Everage. Nor do they have a selection of glamour clothes hidden away on the top of the wardrobe for dressing-up purposes. For transsexuals, the clothes are not really all that important, and most are not noticeably fashion-conscious. The most important thing is that they no longer have the hated, alien-seeming sex organs underneath their clothes. They are not simply dressing up as women, or as men; they actually have become, as near as possible with current techniques, members of the gender of their choice.

It is not helpful to consider homosexuals, transvestites and transsexuals together. Most transsexuals feel that they have suffered by being regarded as kinky, along with sexual exhibitionists or fetishists. In fact, transsexualism is not a manifestation of sexual deviancy. The unlovely phrase gender dysphoria in fact sums up the condition more accurately than any other description.

Also, although there is no cure for homosexuality or transvestism, and most practitioners would never want to be cured, transsexuals do desperately want to be relieved of their sufferings. And for them there is a cure – hormones and surgery. Once the body has been adapted to conform to the convictions of the mind, all is usually well. There is no kind of treatment on earth that would 'cure' a homosexual, or which would stop the transvestite from wanting to cross-dress. In each case the 'condition', if seen as such, is part of the individual, and he has no wish to be different. But transsexuals feel that they have been born all wrong, and wish to right themselves. Gays and transvestites are not uncomfortable with themselves, whereas pre-operative transsexuals are often in acute and unbearable agony. A post-operative transsexual is a 'cured' transsexual, whereas there is no such being as a post-treatment gay person or transvestite.

CHAPTER 9

Transsexualism and the battle of the sexes

However much pre-operative transsexuals may feel that they are living out a lie in their original sex, the fact remains that when they eventually change over they find that life is very different on the 'other side' – so much so that they often feel they have entered an alien country for which little in their previous experience has prepared them. They frequently find that the 'real' men and women whose world they enter post-operatively are very different creatures from what they had imagined.

One transsexual told me she found men and women so unalike as to seem almost like members of different species. When I asked her to elaborate, she said that whereas a man had to act, a woman could just be. It was easier to be a woman, in the sense that you did not have to prove yourself or be active in any way, in her view. This particular transsexual said she had come to the conclusion that femininity was the natural, normal state and that masculinity was something added on, something which had to keep being proved.

A man has to prove constantly, to both himself and others, that he is a man, and this involves self-assertion – throwing his weight around in some way. He has to be active and energetic in order to remind himself that he exists. Otherwise he may risk being told, or feel, that he is not a proper man. A woman, by contrast, can just sit or lie around and be completely passive if she likes, without provoking any doubt that she is a woman. She does not have to do anything at all to prove herself. A woman does not even have to perform any of the standard stereotyped feminine activities, such as bearing and looking after children, or cooking, for the world to accept her as a woman. The transsexual who evinced these views was not saying there was necessarily anything better about the man's restless and continuous activity; in fact, she maintained that she hated men for their egotism and arrogance. For her, it was simply a self-evident fact that it is not necessary to do anything to show the world that you are a woman.

This view is, of course, the standard one adopted by psychiatrists and it is also underlined by myths and fairy-tales. Masculinity is seen as the active principle, and femininity is the passive principle. A man does, and a woman has things done to her − either by men, or by other women. Almost every fairy story which has lasted and been universally popular reflects man's activity and woman's passivity. The most popular story in the whole world, in every single culture and society, apparently, is *Cinderella*, in some form or other. In this tale the heroine represents an absolute form of passivity. She is kept in subjection and virtual slavery by her two ugly sisters who, although nominally women, are considered to have rejected that rôle owing to their ugliness and unwomanly behaviour. Therefore, nobody will love them.

Cinderella's father, in most versions, is a weak man, while the fairy godmother, who is female, enables Cinderella to go to the ball. So there is also an active female and a passive male. But of course the fairy godmother only has a limited influence, at night but always before midnight. At that moment her power vanishes. Even after the fairy godmother has visited her, Cinderella's life can never change permanently until she meets Prince Charming at the ball, who then falls in love with her and in due course whisks her away to a happier life. Cinderella's very passivity and powers of patient endurance enable her to live happily in the end. Almost all other nursery stories rely on a similar principle: eventually, the handsome prince comes to rescue the damsel in distress. She is never able to rescue herself. Little Miss Muffet hasn't even got the gumption to stand on the spider: instead, it frightens her away. Rapunzel is locked up by a wicked witch in a tall tower, and though she can grow her hair long enough to make a ladder for the prince to come, she cannot escape by her own efforts. Only a man can frustrate the power of the witch.

The Sleeping Beauty can only be awakened by a man's kiss, and Little Red Riding Hood is saved by the woodcutter who arrives just in time to prevent her being devoured by the wolf.

In Greek myth, Croesus causes his daughter Danae to be locked up in a brass tower so that the prophesy of her having a son who will later kill him cannot be fulfilled. Of course, Danae nevertheless has a son, fathered by Zeus, who comes to her in the form of a shower of gold. The son, Perseus, grows up to be very active indeed, stealing the one eye from the three otherwise blind Graeae sisters and killing the Gorgon. Danae is the passive instrument that enables the prophecy to be fulfilled. In most versions of the myth, she does not even seem to speak or have any thoughts, and certainly there is no indication that she resists being locked in the brass tower, that she does not welcome Zeus' advances, or that she does anything to stop herself and the baby Perseus from being cast adrift in a trunk. Later, when Danae marries a king, he falls in love with her, rather than the other way round. Penelope, it will be remembered, sits patiently embroidering and unpicking for twenty years so as to remain faithful to her husband Odysseus. She does nothing, while suitors flock to her.

In another myth, Grizelda remains patient while her husband inflicts untold horrors on her to test her. In almost every archetypal tale, women are the objects, men the subjects, the active ones. Passivity in this context must not, however, be confused with weakness, for many mythical women are endlessly enduring, and their stoicism enables destinies to be fulfilled, the good to be rewarded and the evil to be punished. By their very powers of passivity, of putting up with things, these women manage to be the force by which good ultimately triumphs. But, by and large, they are not able to initiate change by their own actions.

If we move from myth to the 'real' world, it is the case that in almost every country in the world males are considered to be superior to females. Men are active, venturing forth to face the world, while women stay put, rooted to their homes and anchored by children or circumstances. Women exist in a secondary, supportive rôle, both in the home and at work, where they tend to be secretaries, receptionists and assistants, rather than initiators – with few exceptions. Commentators such as Germaine Greer have stated that the position of women the world over is actually worse now than it was twenty years ago, and this has been backed up by the volume of essays *Women: A World Report* published by the United Nations in 1984 to mark the end of their decade for women. The feminist movement and the efforts of liberationists have not significantly affected the concept of male activity and female passivity.

Though transsexuals are somehow managing to cross the sex border, and are doing it in ever-increasing numbers, it does not seem that they are enabling the sexes to come together or to become more alike in any way. On the face of it, it appears that transsexuals are a special ultra-minority whose experience bears little relationship to that of ordinary people. But if they can change over, and become very effective 'constructed' men and women, whose secret few can guess, why is there still such a wide gap? Janice Raymond goes some way towards answering this in *The Transsexual Empire*. Her view is that transsexuals are actually *contributing* to the continuing gap between the sexes by reinforcing sex stereotypes in the gender-identity clinics, and then living them out after they have changed over. The transsexual experience, she says, makes us aware how far apart the sexes are and, also, how very much we judge people on their physical appearance. Transsexuals show us, she states, that we judge people as men or women first, and human beings second. If this were not the case, there would be no need for transsexuals to go through the humiliating and mutilating procedures which precede a sex-change. Raymond speaks of a 'zoom lens' effects which concentrates bodily appurtenances and uses these to represent and define the whole essence of maleness and femaleness. This essence is seen, above all, to reside in the secondary sexual characteristics. Once transsexuals have acquired the characteristics of their choice, rather than the ones nature imposed on them, they can then be, to all intents and purposes, 'real' members of their chosen gender. The fact that they are not biological members of the new sex hardly matters at all. The appurtenances are everything.

Raymond argues that while we continue to judge people largely in terms of whether they possess penises or breasts, the sexes will never come together and the present stereotypes, which work so badly against women, will remain. Raymond considers that male-to-female transsexuals are doing the feminist cause no good at all, as they keep pretending to be genuine women and then try to live as traditionally as possible. Raymond states that patriarchy defines our concepts of maleness and femaleness, and that according to this system it is impossible to be neuter. One has to be immediately recognizable as a man or a woman. As things are, we are defined mainly by possession of a certain set of external organs, or a certain body-shape.

We should, ideally, in Raymond's view, be moving towards a state of androgyny, or personhood, whereby a human being is judged primarily on personal qualities rather than body-shape. If transsexuals, who after all have more of the 'other' sex in them than most of us, could accept their androgyny, and even be proud of it, the present wide disparity between the sexes would start to diminish, she claims. Transsexuals are the only people who could point the way, and could teach us much if they were not so desperate to repudiate everything they possibly can about their original sex. While gender-identity clinics exist, however, this can never happen. Transsexualism, according to Raymond, is a stunted attempt at whole-person integrity, a way of becoming a physical hybrid so that male and female qualities can meet in the same person. We could all benefit from taking on board the best of maleness and femaleness, but while transsexualism exists this is impossible, according to Raymond's argument.

It would be good if maleness and femaleness could meet in the same person without that person being gay, or butch, transvestite or dykey. All these labels perpetuate

171

the idea that people must be differentiated by sex before any other aspects of their life or personality can be revealed. Raymond sees male-to-female transsexuals not as real women but as deviant males, and in the sex-rôle stereotyping of our present society this means that a schizoid state has been produced. At the moment, the only people who can identify with transsexuals are other transsexuals. At present, they teach us nothing except this over-awareness of the physical body. Transsexuals tell us that our society places overriding importance on body-shape, and that this is all that seems to matter.

For all their efforts, transsexuals never really enter one world and leave another, but are eternally trapped between, thereby constituting a sort of third sex, one which finds it difficult to relate to either the female or the male world. They are interlopers in their new sex, partly because they have not grown up with the conditioning which affects all biological members of that sex. Transsexuals themselves, on the whole, do not want to bridge the gap between the sexes, but prefer to align themselves wholeheartedly with the sex of their choice.

Janice Raymond is not, as is clear, sympathetic to the transsexual condition, pointing out that many feminists do not welcome these 'constructed' females in their midst. By aligning themselves mainly with the stereotype, they are setting back, rather than furthering, harmony between the sexes. Transsexuals are people who, above all, have found life unlivable in their original sex. By pressing for and demanding surgical mutilation, they reinforce our convictions that the bodily appurtenances are truly vital, and constitute the main differences between the sexes. It is only once their bodies have changed that transsexuals feel they have actually *become* women, or men.

The question remains: is there more to the differences between the sexes than mere body-shape and the organs which determine the reproductive rôle? Are men really active and women passive (with few exceptions) or is this concept something which is foisted on to men and women once their gender has been perceived at birth? We have seen how nature differentiates between males and females at the moment of conception, with the chromosomes. Once the chromosomal orientation is known, the appropriate hormones, in due course, start to encourage the sex organs to develop in either a male or a female fashion. Later, the brain is also influenced by the production of male or female hormones. There is usually no argument about the sex of a baby, which can be determined by the most cursory glance on the part of the midwife. From the point that the parents are told, 'It's a girl', or 'It's a boy', they will start to treat the baby accordingly. Later, all kinds of conditions will set in. Although the male and female sex organs are very similar to each other while the baby is still in the womb, major physical differentiations are made later, and especially after puberty. Reproductively, the sexes cannot change rôles, however much they might want to.

The production of male or female hormones produces not just outward changes, but differences in physical ability. Men are usually physically stronger than women, especially in short-duration challenges, while women perform better in endurance feats. Men are therefore the best sprinters, hurdlers and boxers, while women are pre-eminent at swimming long distances, such as across the English Channel. These different physical attributes are reflected in the myths – men are active, but only for a short period at a time, and women endure, for long stretches. In the case of food shortage or famine, women can last far longer than men; they can also survive for longer in cold conditions. They are built for physical endurance, whereas men are showy, but soon worn out. There is not necessarily any superiority in either attribute, but it is something that certain transsexuals have noticed when undergoing hormone treatment. When women take male hormones, they become physically stronger, while men taking female hormones gain more stamina.

However, these physical attributes are by no means absolute, or universally found. Though men are on the whole larger than women, an average American or Nordic woman is often far bigger, taller and stronger than a Chinese or Korean man. Men from the Far East are only larger than the women of their own race.

When transsexuals go to gender-identity clinics, or are assessed on their marriageability or otherwise, the whole question of their sexual performance suddenly becomes important. Psychiatrists cannot understand why male-to-female transsexuals want vaginas if not for sexual intercourse, and why female-to-male transsexuals should want a penis if not to put it to active use. This aspect of transsexual treatment underlines how very important sexual intercourse is generally held to be in the context of assessing whether a person is serious about transformation. In crude terms, a man is often judged as a man by his ability to penetrate a women, whereas a woman's femininity is frequently assessed on her willingness or enthusiasm for the sexual act. Very often, transsexuals are told they are not serious about wanting to change over unless they tell the psychiatrist that they want to enjoy a full and active sex life in the new rôle. We as a society judge men and women on how they perform sexually in relation to each other, and this has become part of the definition of a functioning member of a particular sex. Transsexuals who say they are not interested in sexual relationships are regarded with suspicion and mistrust. This attitude, which is prevalent at all gender-identity clinics, means than men and women are never seen as autonomous individuals, but only in relation to each other. A woman is a 'real' woman if she relates sexually to men. A man is a 'real' man when he wants to have sexual intercourse with women. A male-to-female transsexual who admits to being a lesbian, and will, after the operation, want to continue to have intimate relationships with other women, may be refused treatment if this is admitted during psychiatric assessment. It is as if men and women were currently seen as only half-people, who need to be completed by a permanent partner of the other sex. Society on the whole sees the sexes only in relation to each other. However, the study of transsexualism enables the light in which men and women are currently regarded, and the different ways they are treated, to become crystal clear. It is assumed that the sexes are very different, that they bear little relationship to each other, and that to cross over the sex border is a very big journey indeed. The average transsexual, at least in the past, believed this idea totally and held that there are major and permanent differences between the sexes. But is this really so? We can see for ourselves that male and female bodies turn out very differently, but has this any significance beyond the requirements of reproduction?

As far as mental qualities are concerned, there seems to be little to choose between the sexes. Intelligence is, as far as we can ascertain, pretty evenly distributed. Men and women also appear to have equal abilities to feel and express joy, sorrow, anger, depression, elation, surprise, humour and so on. Men seem to be more aggressive, arrogant and egotistical and women to be more prone to dependency and attachment, but it is difficult to say how far these qualities are innate and how far they are the result of conditioning. Certainly, they do not seem to be aligned to production of male or female hormone. Everybody knows aggressive women and passive, dependent, helpless men, though presumably these individuals are still producing standard amounts of the hormone appropriate to their biological sex.

The whole subject is very complicated, and as yet nobody knows for sure what the real differences between the sexes are, apart from the physical attributes. It is probable that there are none, that men and women are equally capable of both running multinational companies, organizing wars, coping with machinery and looking after babies or cooking. Either sex can take on the rôle of the other, though there will always be a wide range of individual differences. Everybody has an individual capacity, and not everybody is equally gifted or equally intelligent, but, in the main, human abilities are not inextricably sex-linked. Women have not significantly achieved in the outside world, in comparison with men, but there is nothing to suggest that this is because they do not possess the ability. A great many women have been talented artists, writers and musicians, but they have, in the main, been prepared to give this up to service a man and raise his children. In the past, women have not perceived that they had the choice of carrying on with their careers, but had to give them up as soon as marriage or children came along. As Andrea Dworkin has said, the nearest women could get to becoming barristers, doctors or company directors was to marry them. This is now changing to some extent, but are transsexuals helping or hindering the change? Certainly male-to-female transsexuals themselves continue to achieve, and rarely – if ever – give up their careers or utilize their talents to service and look after a man. But, as Dora observed in an earlier chapter, transsexuals have the advantage in that they have not been conditioned into dependency from their earliest years. Though the male-to-female ones may have perceived themselves as feminine, they were nevertheless brought up in a standard male world. They do not make the mistake of expecting that a man will come and care for them and that henceforward all their worries will be over.

The transsexual experience teaches us that though there may be many perceived differences between the sexes, these are probably more apparent than real, and have to do with physical appearance far more than behaviour, attitudes or abilities. Even the most avowedly masculine man can turn into a very acceptable woman, if the desire is strong enough. The experiences of many male-to-female transsexuals have shown us that once they look like women and are outwardly indistinguishable from women they can do almost exactly as they like and nobody will question their behaviour. Though Janice Raymond states that transsexuals all accept the stereotype without question, I have actually never met one who in my opinion conforms to the 'standard' picture of a man or a woman, assuming that standard picture might encompass a three-bedroom villa, a safe job, two children, a mortgage, a small family saloon and a foreign holiday once a year, with the father being the breadwinner and provider and the woman the housewife, cook and cleaner. Once transsexuals become post-operative, they always have to redefine and modify their relationships with others.

Their experience shows us that men and women can be transformed into surgical constructs of the other, and that, once completed, these constructions can be very convincing. If their stories and dilemmas teach us anything, it is not so much what the basic differences between the sexes are as the overriding importance our society places on appearance. We will accept without question somebody presenting herself as a woman, if he/she looks exactly like a woman. If this person also possesses real breasts, has no male organs, no body and facial hair and plenty of hair on the head, we will see him/her as female. The assumption we make on body-shape will be endorsed if the person carries a handbag, wears make-up, nylons, high heels and a dress. We would only see such a person as a man if the whole presentation was obviously drag. But if it were done for real, and even if the person had big hands and feet and a deep voice, we would unquestioningly accept him/her as female. Once we have accepted the outward, bodily reality of the 'woman', this woman can then behave how she likes.

Once we know she is a woman, we will not think her less of one if she is adept with car engines, can fly an aeroplane or is a computer genius. For although such abilities may be comparatively rare in women, they are by no means unknown. There is no getting away from it: appearance is all. It is the prime hurdle, as gender-identity clinics and SHAFT understand. SHAFT says in its literature that the most important aspect of the change-over is to be able to pass in close, continuous contact with others without any obvious giveaways. Once the visual side has been carefully attended to, little else matters.

The male-to-female transsexual does not have to under-line the new status further by getting married, setting up home as a 'wife', feigning interest in cookery or fashion, or by pretending to be helpless and incompetent. Once a transsexual can successfully 'pass' as a woman, then she has made it. After all, we all know biological women who hate cooking, who are not even slightly interested in clothes and make-up, and who don't want to get married or have children. We also all know of 'real' women who head business empires, and who will stand no nonsense from anybody.

There are many, many women who do not conform to the standard stereotype, but we do not therefore consider them fake women. We do not see world leaders such as

Mrs Thatcher and Mrs Gandhi as men, just because they happened to be premiers of their countries. Because they look feminine, we accept them as women, even though we know that their behaviour is largely indistinguishable from that of a male politician.

Similarly with female-to-male transsexuals, so long as their appearance accords with what we currently find acceptable in a male, they will excite no undue interest, whatever their profession or interests. We might find it slightly odd to discover an apparently normal, masculine man sitting knitting, but it is not unknown. A recent story featured on television concerned a vicar who not only knitted but designed original knitwear for sale. This did not cause viewers to conclude that he was really a woman. If a female-to-male transsexual dresses like a man and has a convincingly deep voice, then he will not have to prove himself further by always being underneath cars, mending fuses or going to football matches. None of the f-to-ms I spoke to for this book were ridiculously masculine, either in their behaviour or in their profession, but were following jobs which could have easily been done by either sex.

What transsexuals prove conclusively is that we judge people primarily on their appearance, then slot them into a category. It doesn't matter all that much if their subsequent behaviour doesn't accord with that catergory in every respect. Once we are satisfied as to which sex they are, the rest is less important. The people we feel most nervous about, apart from those who are actually mentally disturbed, are those we cannot slot into the male or female mould.

This deep desire to slot people into male or female pigeonholes before we can relate to them starts very early in life. When my elder son was four, and met a male-to-female transsexual for the first time, his immediate, embarrassing question was: 'Mummy, is that a man or a lady?' Two years later, when my younger son had attained the same age of indiscretion, he asked the identical question. The 'lady' who put out such confusing signals had blonde hair and lipstick, but wore a mechanic's overalls. If a person's appearance means that it is almost impossible to tell which sex they are supposed to be, we find it extremely difficult to relate to them at all. Until we know whether the individual is male or female, communication is very difficult. For Janice Raymond, this is infinitely regrettable, but for the moment, it persists.

An interesting experiment undertaken by a female journalist proved just how strongly we judge people on their appearance. Celia Brayfield, a successful novelist and journalist, is all woman and has no wish whatever to be a man. She does not resemble a female-to-male transsexual in any respect. But she wondered whether, given the right clothes and professional make-up, she could pass for a day as a man without any raised eyebrows or awkward questions being asked. She was lucky in one respect, in that, at 5 foot 10, she had the height to suspend a certain amount of disbelief.

In her account of her day as a man, published in the *Mail on Sunday*'s *YOU Magazine*, Celia Brayfield wrote:

Life as a man had two major, immediate disappointments; one was that no matter how I combed my hair I didn't look remotely like George Michael. This was a blow. If a thing is worth doing it's worth doing well, and I felt that if I had to be a man I should at least be an attractive one.

The second great let-down was that I was no longer tall. As soon as I put on the jacket, shirt and trousers I had a distinct sense of physical diminishment, as if I'd drunk Alice in Wonderland's shrinking medicine. As a woman of 5 feet 10 inches I was accustomed to being – well – striking; as a man at that height I was merely average. Just putting on the suit transformed me from an amazon to a wimp. These were the first of a series of jolts to my self-perception which made me realize what a different life the other half lives.

A jacket is a wonderful garment, less like an article of clothing than a living environment. With its four inside pockets, multiple change pockets and architectural construction, my jacket felt like a protective shell and a portable home . . . Uncomfortable as it was [Celia had a false beard stuck on with spirit gum, hair by hair] my disguise was completely convincing. My first stop was the Zanzibar, a chic (or posey, depending on your viewpoint) Covent Garden cocktail club where, as a woman, I often call for a restoring margarita or two. As a bearded stranger I boldly signed the member's book in my own name and strode nervously up to the bar. No one gave me so much as a second glance.

'Would you like that table?' asked a surprisingly agreeable waitress eagerly. As a woman I had been used to standing around the bar jockeying for elbow room. It was a new experience to be seated so quickly and pleasantly . . .

Professional acquaintances and personal friends passed me by as they would any other undistinguished bearded-looking bloke. One of my oldest friends . . . saw my name in the register and looked for me in the expensive gloom, but failed to spot a familiar face under the second skin of gauze and bristle: the deception was complete . . .

My voice, which is soft even for a woman, proved no problem provided I spoke loudly and did not smile . . . I found that as a man I was expected to talk in a way which would have been interpreted as harsh, or downright rude, as a woman.

Celia Brayfield went on to say that she soon noticed that people do not look at men at all, and that nobody made any kind of eye contact. She was simply ignored – a new experience. She continued:

People gave me an unusual amount of space physically, as well as psychically. In the rush hour in the City, on crowded pavements or on the Underground, people were reluctant to crowd me, thought twice about opening newspapers in my face and seemed unusually good about not treading on my well-armoured toes. After a while I realized that this extra respect was inspired by fear – fear that aggression would be aroused or that intimacy would be implied by contact.

Driving as a man was a very much improved experience. In my rusty old Renault 12 it was difficult to command respect as a woman, but as a man I found the road miraculously clearer and thronged with other drivers who waved me on matily or acknowledged that my desire to sneak into a traffic jam was perfectly reasonable. Best of all was the experience of breezing confidently out of a blind corner into our local high street which is normally, for women drivers, a kind of motorists'*oubliette*, where one can languish forever, walled in by traffic. As a man, I found I did not need to inch out and force a bus to stop – other, male, drivers let me pass.

Some casual relationships were transformed by a change of sex. Policemen responded to me with a kind of matey, George Dixon respect instead of a patronizing flirtatiousness. Waitresses stepped livelier, barmen were brisker, but waiters were undeniably harder to attract . . . Men do not look at other people in restaurants or anywhere else; I discovered that certain lines of behaviour fazed people and fogged their expectations. Even people in on the secret freaked if I patted my hair or fiddled with my cuff buttons, because these gestures were quintessentially feminine.

Concluding her day-in-a-life-as-a-man, Celia Brayfield wrote:

I found that living as a man was rather like living in a plastic bubble as far as relationships were concerned. A man's world seemed a harsh, lonely place where most relational behaviour was mysteriously taboo. I felt cut off from other people, distanced from them simply by the assumptions they made about manhood. As a person I had a sense of pitching from further back, needing to be louder and tougher in order to be acknowledged.

All Celia Brayford had done was to change her appearance. She didn't consciously behave differently from usual, but was soon aware that she was treated very differently. She discovered that the clothes make the man – and that nobody at all suspected there was a woman underneath. As she says, even the voice was not the giveaway she might have expected.

She spent a day doing exactly the same things she might have done as a woman without making any conscious attempt to act 'manly', but soon discovered two important truths: first, that the world responded to her in a completely new way, and secondly, that after a time the masculine clothes actually started to influence her behaviour. She began to feel like a man and act like a man, with more confidence, more aggression, less interraction and more distance. Despite being a woman who has, presumably, been subjected to the usual kind of female conditioning, Celia Brayfield found that, in men's clothes, it soon became quite natural to act as most people perceive a man.

Janice Raymond hopes that soon transsexuals may be able to accept themselves in their original body-shape and consciously learn to become whole people while remaining in their original biological gender. At the moment, this seems a vain hope indeed, as long as we judge people so completely on their outward appearance. Whatever the inner reality, most transsexuals consider they are living a lie until their bodies can be changed. Whether or not they can become fully functioning men or women in the new sex is largely immaterial. They *look* right, therefore they will be treated as members of the new sex and will respond appropriately – at least, after a short learning period. Because of their understanding of this fact, most transsexuals are never satisfied until they have achieved the fullest surgical reconstruction they can get. This does not mean that they have to look excessively masculine or feminine, but simply that their appearance means there is no doubt, so far as the world is concerned, about their sex.

When transsexuals try to 'pass' successfully as men or women, and when they try to hide their background they are, as Rachael Webb says, denying the reality of their transsexual condition. Rachael Webb has probably done more than any other transsexual to be honest and open about her condition, and hopes that it will enable *all* men and women to share their experiences and come together, rather than being hostile and fearful of each other.

Transsexuals can teach us much about the way in which men and women regard each other – the true, innate differences between the sexes, and to what degree biology and hormones play a part – but only by being prepared to come out and state that they are transsexuals, and by not fearing the world's opinion. At the moment, Rachael Webb's is a lone voice and she is in a minority even within the transsexual minority. If transsexuals try to pretend they are 'real' men and women, simply because they have never felt themselves to be comfortable in their original gender, then they are hiding the validity of their experiences. Transsexuals have also felt in the past that they had to pretend, in case they were shunned by society. Perhaps by now transsexualism has come out into the open enough for more to admit that they are still somewhere between the sexes, and that they still have much of their original sex in them. They should not repudiate their experiences of living in the 'wrong' sex or try to pretend that those years didn't count. They all contributed to making them what they are, and are part of the sum of their life.

Transsexuals are the only people who are in a position to promote harmony between the sexes, from their direct experience. They don't particularly have to make any political statements, just set an example of how it is possible to live successfully as both a man and a woman in the same basic body. Above all, they can demonstrate that what sex you are doesn't matter all that much – it is the person inside the body that really counts.

Bibliography

April Ashley's Odyssey, April Ashley and Duncan Fallowell (Arena, 1983).

Over the Sex Border, Georgina Turtle (Gollancz, 1963).

The Transsexual Phenomenon, Harry Benjamin (The Julian Press, New York, 1966).

The Transsexual Experiment, Robert J. Stoller (The Hogarth Press and The Institute of Psycho-Analysis, 1975).

Transsexualism and Sex Reassignment, edited by Richard Green, MD and John Money, PhD (The Johns Hopkins Press, 1969).

The Transsexual Empire, Janice Raymond (The Women's Press, 1979).

Conundrum, Jan Morris (Coronet, 1975).

Poems of Catullus, translated by Peter Whigham (Penguin Classics, 1966).

Imji Getsul: an English Buddhist in a Tibetan Monastery, Lobzang Jivaka (Routledge, 1962).

Roberta Cowell's Story, Roberta Cowell (Heinemann, 1954).

Variant Sexuality, Research and Theory, edited by Glenn Wilson (Croom Helm, 1987).

The Well of Loneliness, Radclyffe Hall (Corgi, 1974).

Geraldine – For the Love of a Transvestite, Monica Jay (Caliban Books, 1986).

Fascinating Who? Fascinating Aida: the anatomy of a group on the crest of a ripple, mostly by Dillie Keane (Elm Tree, 1986).

A Textbook of Psychosexual Disorders, Clifford Allen (Oxford, 1969).

Gender Dysphoria Syndrome: proceedings of the Second Interdisciplinary Symposium on Gender Dysphoria Syndrome, edited by Donald R. Laub, MD and Patrick Gandy, MS (Sanford University, 1973).